INSIDE LAURA'S LITTLE HOUSE

THE *Little House on the Prairie* TREASURY

By **CAROLYN STROM COLLINS**
and **CHRISTINA WYSS ERIKSSON**

Illustrations by Garth Williams and Cathy Holly

HarperCollins*Publishers*

For our sisters, Elizabeth and Holly
–C.S.C. and C.W.E.

For Renée Graef
–C.H.

Inside Laura's Little House: The *Little House on the Prairie* Treasury
Text copyright © 2000 by Carolyn Collins and Christina Eriksson
New illustrations by Cathy Holly; illustrations copyright © 2000 by Renée Graef
Illustrations from *Little House on the Prairie* copyright © 1953 by Garth Williams
Colorizations were made by Stephen Marchesi with the approval of the Garth Williams estate.
HarperCollins Children's Books, a division of HarperCollins Publishers,
1350 Avenue of the Americas, New York, NY 10019.
www.harperchildrens.com

Library of Congress Cataloging-in-Publication Data
Collins, Carolyn Strom.
  Inside Laura's little house : the Little house on the prairie treasury / Carolyn Strom Collins,
Christina Wyss Eriksson ; illustrations by Cathy Holly and Garth Williams. — 1st ed.
     p.   cm.
  Includes bibliographical references (p. 99) and index.
  Summary: Chapters explore various topics from "Little House on the Prairie," providing
historical and biographical information, recipes, creative activities, and related songs.
    ISBN 0-06-027827-7 — ISBN 0-06-029015-3 (lib. bdg.)
    1. Wilder, Laura Ingalls, 1867–1957. Little house on the prairie—Juvenile literature.   2. Folk
songs, English—Middle West—Juvenile literature.   3. Literary cookbooks—Juvenile literature.
4. Cookery, American—Juvenile literature.   5. Handicraft—Juvenile literature.   [1. Wilder, Laura
Ingalls, 1867–1957. Little house on the prairie.   2. Frontier and pioneer life.   3. Cookery,
American.   4. Handicraft.   5. Songs.]   I. Eriksson, Christina Wyss.   II. Holly, Cathy, ill.
III. Williams, Garth, ill.   IV. Wilder, Laura Ingalls, 1867–1957. Little house on the prairie.
V. Title.
PS3545.I342L5733   2000
813'.52—dc21   99-26797

Typography by Carla Weise
1 2 3 4 5 6 7 8 9 10
❖
First Edition

Acknowledgments

We gratefully acknowledge the help and encouragement of the many people who were willing to share their knowledge and expertise to ensure that this book accurately reflects Laura's life on the prairie:

Brigadier General and Mrs. William Kurtis, present owners of the little house on the prairie; Jeanne Burton, Montgomery County Register of Deeds; and Rick Kemp of the Montgomery County, Kansas, Highway Department.

The University of Missouri Library, Columbia, kindly lent microfilm of Laura's original manuscripts of *Little House on the Prairie* for us to study. Also helpful in our research of the pioneer era in the Midwest were the University of Minnesota Libraries; the Minnesota Historical Society; the Ramsey County and Hennepin County libraries in Minnesota; and the University of Kansas Libraries.

We are very appreciative of the expert guidance of our editors at HarperCollins, Alix Reid and Kara Vicinelli, and our literary agent, Jeanne Hanson.

Cathy Holly has illustrated Laura's experiences on the prairie with exquisite sensitivity and beauty.

We are especially grateful to our husbands, Andy and Mark, for their encouragement and support of this project.

—C.S.C. and C.W.E.

Contents

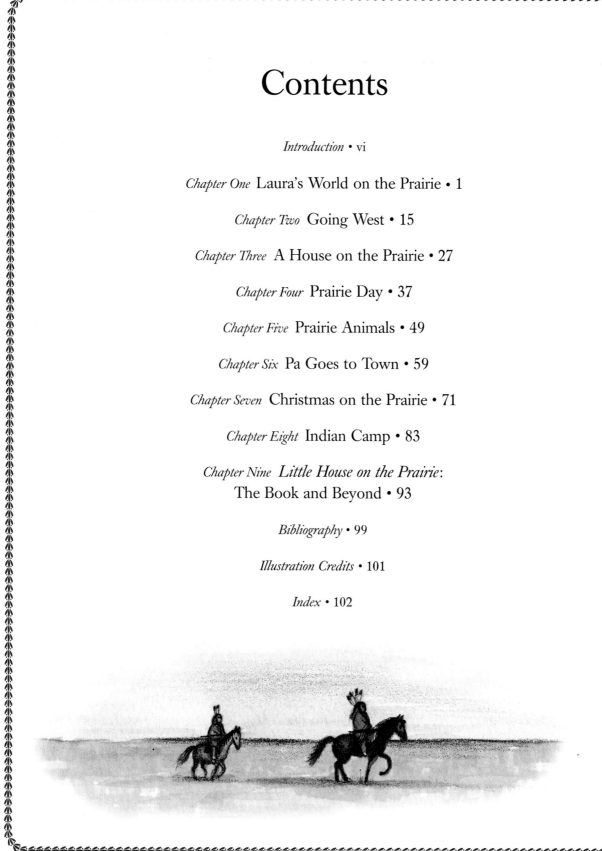

Introduction

Of Laura Ingalls Wilder's nine Little House books, perhaps the most beloved is *Little House on the Prairie*, a heartwarming adventure tale of a little pioneer girl named Laura Ingalls. Few stories can match the excitement of Laura and her family's covered-wagon journey from the Big Woods of Wisconsin to the wide prairies of Kansas and the drama of their experiences as homesteaders on the unsettled frontier.

When we read the Little House books as children and later read them to our own children, we thought about how it might have been to live in those days of log cabins and covered wagons. What was it like to cook every meal over an open fire, to make soap, to sew all the clothes for a family? We also wondered how much of the book was based on actual historical events. Did the neighbors Laura mentioned in the book really exist? Where was Laura's little log cabin, and what did it look like? The more we read, the more we wondered. We began to look for answers to these and other questions that we and our children had about Laura's life on the prairie.

Inside Laura's Little House provides the answers to many of our original questions and to dozens of others we thought of during our research. In the first chapter we provide a biography of Laura's life and a brief summary of *Little House on the Prairie*. We explain how Laura's real life was both different

from and similar to the life she described in the book. We also discuss historic events that occurred during the time Laura lived on the prairie and include a time line and map.

Each of the seven chapters that follow focuses on an important topic from *Little House on the Prairie*, such as traveling west, building a prairie house, and celebrating Christmas on the prairie. In each chapter we summarize the parts of the book that feature that topic, and then we provide more historical details and information related to the topic. In these chapters we also include activities or recipes illustrating some of the things Laura and her family did, such as planting a prairie garden, cooking corn bread, or making paper dolls. And at the end of each chapter there are the words and music to one of the many songs featured in *Little House on the Prairie* or another popular song of the era.

The last chapter of this book is about how *Little House on the Prairie* and the other Little House books came to be published and what Laura thought about their success. We also explain how the book continues to live on today. Compiling all this information about Laura and *Little House on the Prairie* required a great deal of research, and at the end of the book is a bibliography that lists the titles of many of the resources we consulted.

With each new discovery we made about Laura and the way she lived, we increased our measure of respect for the Ingallses and the other pioneers who settled the prairies of the Midwest. Throughout *Little House on the Prairie* the Ingallses endured hardships but remained optimistic and cheerful and created a pattern for living admired and envied by future generations. We hope *Inside Laura's Little House* will make it possible for readers who love Laura and *Little House on the Prairie* to learn more about her life on the frontier—and to be inspired by the self-reliance and determination of a remarkable pioneer girl and an even more remarkable woman.

(Above) Laura Ingalls Wilder around 1906.

(Opposite, left) Wedding photograph of Caroline Quiner and Charles Ingalls, February 1, 1860.

(Opposite, right) From left to right, Carrie, Mary, and Laura.
This is the first photograph ever taken of the three girls.

1

Laura's World on the Prairie

Laura Ingalls Wilder

Laura Ingalls Wilder was born on February 7, 1867, in a log cabin deep in the Big Woods near the frontier town of Pepin, Wisconsin. Her father, Charles Phillip Ingalls, and her mother, Caroline Quiner Ingalls, had come to live in the Big Woods four years earlier, and Laura's sister Mary had been born there in 1865.

The Ingalls family left the Big Woods when Laura was just over a year old, looking for new opportunities in lands being opened up for settlement in the West. This was the first of many moves. Over a period of eleven years their travels took them from Wisconsin to Missouri and Kansas, then back to Wisconsin; to Minnesota and northern Iowa, then back to Minnesota; and finally to De Smet, South Dakota—all before Laura was twelve years old. During this time, three more children were born into the family—Carrie, Grace, and Charles Frederick. Sadly, Freddie died in infancy.

1

Whenever possible, Laura attended school in one-room schoolhouses that dotted the prairie. When she was fifteen, she earned her teacher's certificate and began teaching. She also earned money for the family as a seamstress.

When Laura was eighteen, she married Almanzo Wilder, who was ten years older than she. Almanzo had grown up in New York State and had moved west with his family when he was a teenager; he had come to the De Smet area about the same time as the Ingallses.

Laura and Almanzo settled near De Smet on their own claim. Their daughter, Rose, was born there a year later in 1886. They lived in De Smet for about nine years, with short stays in Minnesota and Florida.

In 1894 Laura, Almanzo, and Rose left De Smet for good and journeyed by covered wagon to Mansfield, Missouri, where they bought a piece of land they named Rocky Ridge. They cleared the land, planted hundreds of apple trees, and eventually made Rocky Ridge into a family farm. Over

(Above) Laura at age seventeen, in 1884.

(Right) Almanzo as a young De Smet homesteader.

(Below) Rose Wilder, around four years old.

a period of about twenty years, Laura and Almanzo built a large white farmhouse to replace the log cabin in which they started out. Laura and Almanzo never moved again.

In addition to her duties on Rocky Ridge farm, Laura wrote newspaper articles and a magazine column about a woman's life on the farm for *The Missouri Ruralist*. In the 1930s Laura began writing down her memories of her childhood. Her stories, known as the Little House books, immediately became classics, and Laura's books have been enjoyed by millions of readers all over the world ever since.

(Above) The Wilder farmhouse.

*(Right) Mr. and Mrs. Almanzo J. Wilder,
the winter after they married.*

*E*arly on a cold late-winter morning, Ma, Pa, Mary, Laura, and Baby Carrie drove their covered wagon slowly away from their log cabin in the Big Woods of Wisconsin and began their long trip over rutted roads and trails to eastern Kansas.

The Ingallses crossed into Kansas in the early summer and immediately started to look for a place to build their home. Pa chose a piece of land with no big trees to cut down or plow around.

Pa immediately began building the cabin with logs he cut by a creek that flowed near the site. He finished the house and dug a deep well with help from prairie neighbors Mr. Edwards and Mr. Scott.

Life on the prairie was pleasant but not easy. The family fought prairie fires and wild animals and malaria, which they called fever 'n' ague. They survived the winter only to discover that the

United States government had not paid the Osage tribe for the land on which the Ingallses and other settlers lived. The Osage were angry, and the settlers were concerned there might be a war. Then an Osage leader named Soldat du Chêne convinced his people not to fight the settlers and to move south instead.

Laura watched the long line of Osage ride past the little house. But because the land the Ingalls family lived on still belonged to the Osage tribe, in the late spring they had to leave too.

Little House on the Prairie *ends with Laura and her family traveling by covered wagon once again, looking for another place to live.*

The Ingallses' Real Life on the Prairie

>>>

Little House on the Prairie is the second book about the Ingalls family in Laura Ingalls Wilder's series of Little House books. The first one, *Little House in the Big Woods*, tells of their life in the Big Woods of Wisconsin, where Laura was born.

Although Laura's account of the Ingallses' life on the prairie is based largely on fact, she found it necessary to change a few things in order to make the transition from the first book to the second one. Laura wrote *Little House on the Prairie* as though the family moved to the prairie when she was six years old, Mary was eight, and Carrie was a baby. But actually the Ingallses left Wisconsin in 1868, when Laura was just over a year old. They moved first to Missouri and lived there for a year before then moving to the prairie in what is now southeastern Kansas. So Laura was really only two years old, and Mary four, when the journey she describes in her book began. And Carrie hadn't even been born yet! She would arrive in the little prairie cabin on August 3 of the following year.

In addition to the girls' ages, Laura also changed the time period covered in *Little House on the Prairie*; she compressed the family's two-year stay on the prairie into a little over one year. In the book they leave Wisconsin in the winter and leave the Kansas prairie the following spring. However, in reality the Ingalls family arrived in Independence in the fall of 1869 and left in spring of 1871.

Although Laura would have been too young to remember most of

what happened in the little prairie house, the stories in *Little House on the Prairie* are true. Ma and Pa had told them so many times around the family hearth that they became part of Laura's own memory.

The characters in *Little House on the Prairie* were real people; the existence of most of them has been confirmed in census and land-claim records. In the book and in real life Dr. George Tann (Laura spelled his name "Tan" in her book), a black physician, treated the Ingalls family when they were ill with malaria. Dr. Tann lived with his parents just north of the Ingallses. The Tann family had come from Pennsylvania to the Kansas prairie in 1869, about the same time as the Ingallses. Dr. Tann, who had received his medical training back east, quickly became known as a fine physician and treated people throughout the area. He lived in Kansas for the rest of his life, and in 1872 he filed for a patent on his own land, not far from his parents' land, built a house, and established a farm. He continued to practice medicine until he was sixty-eight years old, and died in 1909 at the age of seventy-five.

In addition to Dr. Tann, Laura also mentions neighbors Mr. and Mrs. Scott in *Little House on the Prairie.* In the book Mrs. Scott nurses the family back to health after their bout with malaria, and Mr. Scott helps Pa dig the well. Documents verify that the William Scott family lived two miles south of the Ingallses in the Fawn Creek Township, near Onion Creek, and researchers believe they are the Scott family about which Laura wrote.

Unfortunately, Mr. Edwards, one of the most beloved characters from the book and indeed from the entire series, remains a mystery. No one listed in the census or in land records fits Laura's description of him—single and a "wildcat from Tennessee." Like Pa, he must have neglected to file a claim on his land and left the territory before the final settlement with the Osage was made.

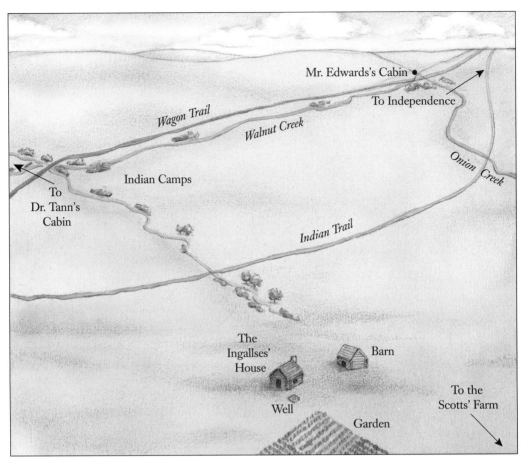

The little house on the prairie.

Another difference between reality and the version Laura wrote about nearly sixty years later was the distance from Independence to the little house. In her book she says several times that Independence was forty miles away; however, the distance is actually only about twelve miles.

For years Laura's assertion in *Little House on the Prairie* that the little house was forty miles away made it difficult to pinpoint the original site. Pa had never filed a formal claim to the land, and by the time Laura wrote her book in the 1930s, the little log cabin he had built had disappeared. Thanks to some detective work by Margaret Clement, Eileen Charbo, and others in

The little house on the prairie replica cabin.

Inside the replica cabin.

the 1960s, the exact site of the little house on the prairie was finally established. Perhaps the most valuable clue to the location of the little house was the line in the Ingalls family Bible that listed Carrie's birthplace and birthday: Montgomery County, Kansas, August 3, 1870. After discovering that Carrie had been born in Montgomery County, the researchers waded through census records and land records and finally determined that the Ingalls house had been built on the southwest quarter of Section 36 in Rutland Township, Montgomery County, Kansas. Today, a replica cabin stands on the site; a well, presumed to be the one Pa and Mr. Scott dug, is nearby.

Laura's Times

In 1869, when the Ingallses arrived in Kansas, the United States was still recovering from the Civil War, which had ended in 1865. This was the period of Reconstruction (1865–1877). The South had been devastated by the war, and the southern states were rebuilding their cities under the rules and regulations of Congress. Northern states were also recovering from the war, but their damages were not as substantial.

Most southern states had ratified the Thirteenth Amendment, abolishing slavery, but they had also created laws that severely limited the rights of African Americans. A disagreement in Congress between radical Republicans and President Andrew Johnson over southern Reconstruction led to the President's impeachment, although he was not convicted. After Johnson's term ended, Ulysses S. Grant, who had led the Union Army to victory in the Civil War, became the eighteenth president in 1869. There were thirty-seven states in the Union at that time.

The years of Reconstruction were marked by westward expansion. The transcontinental railroad, begun in 1862, was finally completed in 1869. On May 10 the ceremony joining the Union Pacific Railroad and the Central Pacific Railroad was held in Utah. This monumental achievement made it possible for passengers and freight to be moved across the country quickly and more efficiently than ever before. As additional railroad lines were built across the West, settlement of the plains grew more and more possible and desirable.

People were also enticed to move west by the Homestead Act of 1862, which gave 160 acres (a quarter square mile) of unoccupied public land to each homesteader who lived on the land and cultivated it for five years. In the late 1860s settlers were moving into newly opened lands west of the Mississippi River, forcing Indian tribes to move even farther west or into areas set aside for them by the government. What is now the state of Oklahoma was known as Indian Territory at that time and was designated land for tribes such as the Cherokee and the Osage.

Many writers were hard at work during Laura's early years, including Louisa May Alcott, Jules Verne, Mark Twain, Harriet Beecher Stowe, and Frances Hodgson Burnett. Those years also marked the beginning of an era full of innovations. Thomas Alva Edison had just begun his remarkable career as an inventor. His first major achievement, in 1869, was the creation of the Edison Universal Stock Printer, the first reliable ticker-tape machine. During the next fifty years Edison created many important inventions that we still use today, including the phonograph in 1877 and the electric light bulb in 1879. Also during the time the Ingallses lived in Kansas, Alexander Graham Bell was beginning to experiment with mechanical means to transmit sounds. By 1876 Bell had been granted a patent for the telephone.

The age of the machine had begun while the Ingallses were living in their one-room log cabin on the prairie, cooking over an open fire, and reading by candlelight.

Time Line 1868–1871

1868

- **The Ingalls family leaves their cabin in the Big Woods of Wisconsin; they travel by covered wagon for two months to settle in Chariton County, Missouri. Laura is one year old; Mary is three.**
- The Osage tribes agree to sell their lands in southern Kansas to the United States government, but the treaty is not finalized until 1872.
- Congress passes the Fourteenth Amendment, which grants citizenship to African Americans.
- The impeachment trial of President Andrew Johnson officially begins.
- Louisa May Alcott's *Little Women* (Part One) is published.
- The lawn mower, the tape measure, and baseball uniforms are introduced.

1869

- **The Ingalls family leaves Missouri; they travel by covered wagon for about a month to settle near the new town of Independence. Laura is two years old; Mary is four.**
- The town of Independence, Kansas, is founded. One of the first buildings in the new town, a hotel called the Judson House, is built. E. E. Wilson and F. D. Irwin open the first store in Independence, and the first issue of the *Independence Pioneer* newspaper is published.

- Dr. George Tann, the physician who will treat the Ingallses for malaria, settles with his parents, Bennet and Mary Tann, near the Ingalls farm in Montgomery County, Kansas.
- Almanzo Wilder is twelve years old and living in Malone, New York.
- Ulysses S. Grant becomes the eighteenth president of the United States.
- Wyoming Territory allows women to vote.
- The transcontinental railroad is completed at Promontory Point, Utah.
- Statesman Mahatma Gandhi is born.
- Louisa May Alcott's *Little Women* (Part Two) is published.
- Postcards and the vacuum cleaner are introduced.

1870

- **On August 3 Caroline Celestia (Carrie) is born in the little house on the prairie; Laura is three years old; Mary is five.**
- Independence's first school opens in April, and the first stagecoach arrives from Oswego.
- Asa Hairgrove begins recording the U.S. Census in Montgomery County, arriving at the Ingalls cabin on August 13; the population of Independence is 435.
- Almanzo Wilder, age thirteen, moves with his family from New York to Spring Valley, Minnesota.
- Congress passes the Fifteenth Amendment, granting the right to vote regardless of race, color, or previous condition of servitude.
- Robert E. Lee, commander of the Confederate Army, and Charles Dickens, author of *A Christmas Carol*, die.
- John D. Rockefeller founds Standard Oil.
- Jules Verne's *20,000 Leagues Under the Sea* is published.
- Congress declares Christmas Day a national legal holiday.

1871

- **Pa receives word that the United States government is planning to evict settlers from Osage lands. In the spring the Ingallses leave the little house on the prairie and begin their trip back to Pepin, Wisconsin. Laura is four years old; Mary is six. That fall Laura attends school for the first time at Barry Corner School in Pepin County.**
- In April the population of Independence reaches 1,382.
- The first railroad line into Independence is completed.
- The city of Chicago is nearly destroyed by a four-day fire.
- The first professional baseball association is formed, the National Association of Professional Base Ball Players.
- *The Wonders of the Animal World* (Pa's "big green animal book") by G. Hartwig is published.
- Stephen Crane, author of *The Red Badge of Courage*, is born.
- Verdi's opera *Aida* debuts.
- Chewing gum is introduced.

A long time ago . . . Pa and Ma and
Mary and Laura and Baby Carrie left their
little house in the Big Woods of Wisconsin.
They were going to the Indian country.

—CHAPTER 1

2

Going West

When Ma and Pa decided to leave the Big Woods, they quickly prepared for the long journey. They sold their little log house and packed their wagon with supplies. Pa made a cover for the wagon by taking young hickory branches, bending them into arches, and fastening each end to the sides of the wagon. He and Ma stretched white canvas over the wooden frame.

After the Ingallses said their good-byes to the friends and relatives who gathered at dawn to see them off, they started the long trip to southern Kansas. There were many adventures along the way—crossing the frozen Mississippi, trading their tired horses for two young mustangs named Pet and Patty, fording a treacherous river, and almost losing Jack, their brindle bulldog. They could cover only about twenty miles a day in the heavy wagon, and they camped every night along the way. At first the journey was exciting, but eventually Laura began to think the weeks on the trail would never end. "Day after day they traveled in Kansas, and saw nothing but the rippling grass and enormous sky."

Finally, the family reached a little plot of land in southeastern Kansas that would become their home for the next year and a half. A new adventure had begun.

Why the Pioneers Went West

Pioneers like Charles and Caroline Ingalls had a number of reasons for deciding to leave their homes and move west to completely unsettled territory. The main reason was that land was cheap and available. The Homestead Act of 1862, passed by the United States Congress when Abraham Lincoln was president, was designed to encourage the settlement of the millions of acres of newly opened lands. Homesteading meant that a person could claim 160 acres of government land just by living on the land for five years and improving it.

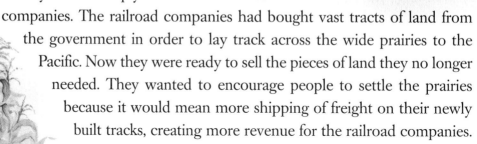

If settlers chose not to homestead, they could buy land cheaply from the railroad companies. The railroad companies had bought vast tracts of land from the government in order to lay track across the wide prairies to the Pacific. Now they were ready to sell the pieces of land they no longer needed. They wanted to encourage people to settle the prairies because it would mean more shipping of freight on their newly built tracks, creating more revenue for the railroad companies.

But inexpensive land wasn't the only reason the West was attractive to so many people. The land was full of natural resources. The rich topsoil of the prairies had never been widely cultivated, so crops grew easily once the thick prairie grass was plowed, and there were plenty of animals for hunting. Fewer people on the land also meant less crowding, less noise, and fewer demands on the land and its resources. All these reasons meant unlimited opportunity to pioneers like the Ingallses.

Of course, even with so much to entice people to move west, many opted to remain in the more developed and populated areas of the East. But hearty souls like Charles Ingalls, who longed for wide-open spaces, packed up their covered wagons, waved good-bye to friends and relatives, and bravely headed for the frontier.

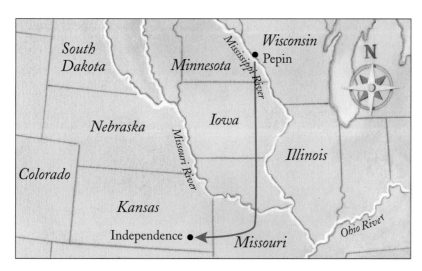

The Ingallses' journey.

Breakfast Bacon

Mary and Laura looked at each other and laughed.
They could smell bacon and coffee and hear pancakes sizzling,
and they scrambled out of bed. —CHAPTER 4

Pioneers like the Ingallses brought bacon with them on their covered-wagon journeys. They wrapped big slabs of dried bacon in layers of paper and put the wrapped bacon into cloth bags, which they hung inside the wagon. When they wanted to cook the bacon, they simply cut thin slices off the slab with a sharp butcher knife and cooked the slices. Although we still can buy slabs of bacon at some butcher shops, bacon today is usually sold in packages, already sliced. To make your bacon like the kind Laura had on the prairie, choose the thicker-sliced variety with as little fat in it as possible.

Do not attempt to cook bacon without adult help, as the hot grease can be dangerous.

To cook slices of bacon, you will need:

2 or 3 slices of bacon per person   *Cooking fork*
Paper towels   *Aluminum foil (optional)*
Several layers of newspaper   *Long-handled cooking spoon*
Heavy skillet (a cast-iron skillet is   *Heat-proof container*
*   the best)*   *Plate*

1. Place a layer of paper towels on top of several layers of newspaper and set aside. You will use these to drain the cooked bacon.
2. Lay a single layer of bacon slices flat in the skillet, slightly overlapping the slices. (If there isn't room in the skillet for all the bacon slices, wait until the

first slices start to cook, then add the rest. The slices will shrink as they cook, making room for more. Keep cooking and adding slices until you have cooked all you need.)

3. Put the skillet on the large burner of the stove and turn the heat to medium.

4. As the bacon begins to brown on the bottom, use the fork to carefully turn over the slices. Stand well away from the skillet as the bacon cooks, because it tends to pop and spatter. You can lay a piece of aluminum foil over the top of the skillet to catch the spatters if you wish.

5. Spoon any excess grease in the skillet into the heatproof container; this will also cut down on the spattering.

6. When the bacon slices are nicely brown, lift them from the skillet with the fork and lay them on paper towels to drain the excess fat.

7. Serve the bacon slices immediately or put them on the plate. Cover the plate with aluminum foil and keep it in a warm oven until ready to serve.

PRAIRIE RECIPES

Ma's Pancakes

*Then they sat on the clean grass and ate pancakes and bacon
and molasses from the tin plates in their laps.* —CHAPTER 4

How Ma managed to make pancakes out on the lonely prairie is a bit of a mystery. Pancakes call for some ingredients that most pioneers did not usually have in their wagons, namely eggs and milk. The eggs may have come from the thousands of prairie chickens that Laura saw running around the campsite. And it is possible that Pa bought milk from a settler nearby.

Pancakes also call for baking powder or yeast or some other form of leavening (an ingredient that makes the batter rise and the pancakes light and fluffy). Pioneers made their own baking powder from bicarbonate of soda (they called it saleratus) and cream of tartar. Many pioneers, including Ma, also kept a crock of sourdough starter on hand that could be used instead of yeast in breads and pancakes.

To make pancakes similar to the ones Ma made, you will need:

1½ cups all-purpose flour	Butter
1½ cups whole-wheat flour	Molasses or maple syrup
½ teaspoon salt	2 large mixing bowls
2 teaspoons baking powder	Mixing spoon
2 eggs	Fork
¼ cup molasses (or brown sugar)	Skillet or griddle
4 cups milk	Pancake turner
3 tablespoons bacon fat or melted butter (plus a bit more for greasing the skillet)	

20

1. Put the flours, salt, and baking powder into one of the large bowls. Mix together with the spoon and set aside.

2. In the other bowl beat the two eggs slightly with a fork. Add the molasses, milk, and 3 tablespoons bacon fat or melted butter to the eggs and stir.

3. Pour the egg mixture into the dry ingredients, and mix until they are just combined. (Do not overmix; it will make the pancakes tough.)

4. Set the batter aside for a few minutes while you prepare the skillet or griddle.

5. Generously grease the skillet with bacon fat. Place the skillet on the stove and turn the heat to medium high.

6. After a few minutes sprinkle a few drops of water on the skillet. If the water sizzles, the pan is hot enough to start cooking the pancakes.

7. Spoon the pancake batter into the hot skillet in any size or shape that you wish.

8. When bubbles start to appear on the surfaces of the pancakes, check to see if the bottoms are browned by lifting up the pancakes a bit with the pancake turner. If the bottoms are browned, turn over each pancake with the pancake turner. Let them cook a few minutes more until they are browned on the other side and cooked all the way through.

9. Serve the pancakes hot with butter. Pour molasses over them (as Laura did) or top them with maple syrup.

THIS RECIPE WILL MAKE ABOUT 24 4-INCH PANCAKES.

Mary and Laura's Nightcaps

Ma helped Mary and Laura undress. She put their long nightgowns over their heads while they stuck their arms into the sleeves. They buttoned the neckbands themselves, and tied the strings of their nightcaps beneath their chins. —CHAPTER 3

When Mary and Laura were children, girls usually wore long night-gowns and nightcaps to bed in winter and summer. The nightcaps kept their heads warm in the winter, kept their long hair clean and tidy, and kept little insects out of it.

There were many styles of nightcaps. The ones Laura and Mary wore had strings that tied under the chin.

To make your own nightcap similar to Mary and Laura's, you will need:

Cotton fabric, 15 × 36 inches	*Needle*
Ruler	*Sewing scissors*
Pins	*Large safety pin*
Iron	*1 yard of ¼-inch-wide ribbon*
Ironing board	*1 yard of ½-inch-wide ribbon*
Matching thread	

1. Hem the two short (15-inch) edges of the fabric. Turn each edge under about ¼ inch, pinning it in a few places if necessary. Press the edge with a warm iron. Turn each edge under again, press, then hand stitch the edges.

¹/₄ inch   *¹/₄ inch*

2. Fold the edges of the two long (36-inch) sides down ¼ inch, then press.

3. Fold one of the long sides down again ¾ inch wide and press. Hand stitch the hem close to the edge. This will form a space called a casing through which the ¼-inch ribbon will go.

4. Fold the other long side down 2 inches and hem it as you did in step 3. Stitch another row ¾ inch from the hem stitches, as shown. This will form a casing for the ½-inch ribbon as well as a ruffle to frame your face.

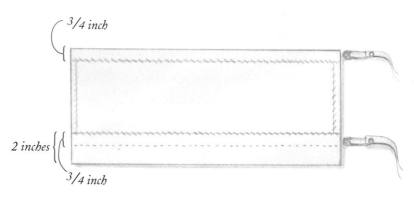

3/4 inch

2 inches

3/4 inch

5. Pin the large safety pin to one end of the ¼-inch-wide ribbon and slide it all the way through the narrow casing. Remove the pin. Adjust the ends of the ribbon so they are equal. Gather the material along the ribbon to form the back of the nightcap. Tie the ribbon ends into a bow.

6. Pin the large safety pin to one end of the ½-inch-wide ribbon and slide it all the way through the wider casing. Remove the pin. Adjust the ends of the ribbon so they are equal. Gather the material along the ribbon to form the ruffled front of the nightcap.

7. Put on the nightcap and tie the front ribbons under your chin. Adjust the front and back gathers to fit your head.

Ma's Soft Soap

Ma brought the wooden pannikin of soft soap from the wagon. . . .
She washed sheets and pillow-cases and white underthings, she washed
dresses and shirts, and she rinsed them in clear water and spread them on the
clean grass, to dry in the sun. —CHAPTER 4

Pioneers usually made their own soap, called hard soap, and they did not throw away even the smallest slivers. They put pieces of the hard soap into a jar or crock and covered them with a little boiling water to soften them. After the bits of soap and water were stirred for a while, they became "soft soap" and could be used up completely. Ma used her wooden pannikin—a small pan or cup—for collecting scraps of hard soap that she later made into soft soap.

To make your own soft soap, you will need:

Slivers of soap, enough to half fill the
cup or can (collect almost-used-up
bars of soap from around the
house, or shave off bits of soap
with a vegetable peeler)

1 small cup or can
2 tablespoons hot water
Spoon

1. Put the bits of soap into the cup. When the cup is half filled with soap, pour 2 tablespoons of hot water into the cup.

2. Stir the soap and water slowly until the soap begins to soften and melt. Let the mixture stand for at least 2 hours or overnight.

3. Stir the mixture again. The soft soap should be thick, almost like jelly. If the soap is too thick, add more hot water, a few drops at a time. If it is too thin, add more pieces of soap and let the mixture stand for another few hours to soften.

4. Your soap is ready to use! To make it last, add scraps of soap and hot water as often as you wish.

PRAIRIE SONGS

Oh! Susanna

Softly Pa's fiddle sang in the starlight. Sometimes he sang a little and sometimes the fiddle sang alone. —CHAPTER 4

"Oh! Susanna" was a favorite song of pioneers. It was written by Stephen Foster, a composer well known for many other tunes, including "My Old Kentucky Home" and "Camptown Races."

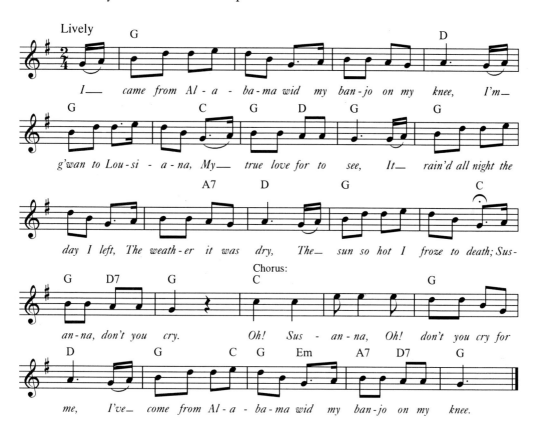

Lively

G ... D

I— came from Al - a - ba-ma wid my ban-jo on my knee, I'm—

G ... C G D G ... G

g'wan to Lou-si - a - na, My— true love for to see, It— rain'd all night the

A7 D G C

day I left, The weath-er it was dry, The— sun so hot I froze to death; Sus-

G D7 G C G (Chorus:)

an-na, don't you cry. Oh! Sus - an-na, Oh! don't you cry for

D G C G Em A7 D7 G

me, I've— come from Al - a - ba-ma wid my ban-jo on my knee.

$\mathscr{P}$a carefully took the

nails one by one from his mouth,

and with ringing blows of the hammer

he drove them into the slab.

—CHAPTER 10

3

A House on the Prairie

When the Ingallses reached the spot Pa had chosen for their little house, Pa wasted no time getting started on the family's cabin. As soon as he and Ma had unloaded the wagon, Pa drove down to the creek and began to cut down trees. He brought back load after load of logs.

Pa started working on the house alone, but when the walls were three logs high, he needed help. Ma worked alongside Pa until one of the heavy logs slipped and fell on her foot. For days Ma's foot was too painful and swollen for her to help Pa. But one day Pa came home from hunting and announced he had met a neighbor, Mr. Edwards, who would help him finish building.

The next day Pa and Mr. Edwards finished all four walls, cut out two windows and a door, and put a skeleton roof on top. But the log cabin wasn't finished. Pa built a stable for the horses and then he finished the cabin—he put on a slab roof, laid a puncheon floor, and put in the windows and a door. He built a fireplace and chimney, and later he made beds to sleep on, chairs to sit on, and a table to eat from. He even dug a well so the family would have fresh water nearby.

Finally, the little log cabin was complete. Laura was thrilled "to be living in a house again."

27

Prairie Homes

The first thing every homesteader had to do when he reached his claim was to build a house on the site. Not only was a house necessary to provide shelter from the weather and wild animals, it was also a requirement by the government.

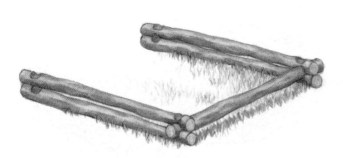

According to the Homestead Act, the house had to be at least fourteen feet by sixteen feet (about the size of an average room in today's homes). Pioneers like Charles Ingalls did not have measuring tapes to measure the house exactly, but as Laura said, they "paced off the size of it on the ground." A giant step would equal about three feet, so Pa could guess pretty easily about the size of the house; about five giant steps wide and six giant steps long would more than fulfill the minimum requirement.

Some pioneers like the Ingallses knew how to build cabins, dig wells, and do all the other tasks that needed to be done to make a homestead. Charles Ingalls had been pioneering since he was a boy and could be considered an expert. Other pioneers were not so well informed; they were called tenderfeet and had to learn from the more experienced settlers.

Pioneers like the Ingallses did most of the work on their land themselves. They built their cabins from materials they found close by, from trees that grew along the creeks, or from bales of prairie grass or hay, or from blocks of

sod cut out of the prairie. Neighbors often helped each other with some of the harder tasks, like building the log walls high enough to make the roof and digging a well deep enough to reach fresh water.

Once the cabin was built, furniture was needed. Some settlers brought a few pieces of furniture with them in their covered wagons; others, like the Ingalls family, made simple tables, chairs, beds, and other pieces.

There were no electric wires to run into a pioneer cabin, no plumbing pipes or fixtures to install, and no furnace. Light came from sunshine or moonlight when the sky was clear; the fireplace and candles also gave some light to the one-room cabin. Water for drinking, cooking, and washing came from the creek or the well, one pail at a time. A chamber pot kept under the bed or an outhouse several yards away from the cabin was the only sort of toilet anyone of that era knew, pioneer or city dweller. The fireplace at one end of the cabin provided heat for cooking and for warmth in the cold winters.

Laura wrote that the Ingallses loved their little prairie house. It was home to the well-traveled family, for "the red-checked cloth was on the table, the little china woman glimmered on the mantel-shelf, and the new floor was golden in the flickering firelight." Even without the luxuries that we think of now as necessities, life in the little house on the prairie was cozy and full of promise.

PRAIRIE RECIPES

Ma's Jackrabbit Stew

Pa held up the game in his hand, for Laura to see.
He had a rabbit, the largest rabbit she had ever seen,
and two plump prairie hens. —CHAPTER 4

After Mr. Edwards and Pa spent the whole day building the cabin, they were hungry! Pa and Ma invited Mr. Edwards to eat supper with them, and Ma served a fine supper of jackrabbit stew, "steaming-hot, thick cornbread flavored with bacon fat," molasses, and coffee sweetened with brown sugar.

Below and on the next page are recipes for jackrabbit stew and dumplings. Make both recipes at the same time so you can serve them together.

To make jackrabbit stew, you will need:

½ cup flour
1 teaspoon salt
1 teaspoon ground pepper
3 pounds rabbit, cut into serving
pieces (you can buy rabbit at
many grocery stores or substitute
chicken pieces if you prefer)
2 tablespoons shortening or lard
1 onion, sliced

3 carrots, sliced (optional)
2 potatoes, peeled and diced (optional)
4 cups chicken broth
1 teaspoon apple cider vinegar
Baking pan
Large pot (5 quarts or more) with
a lid
Tongs or long-handled fork
Long-handled spoon

1. Mix the flour, salt, and pepper in the pan.

2. Roll the pieces of rabbit in the flour mixture until they are well coated on all sides. Set aside.

3. Melt the shortening in the pot over medium-high heat.

4. Put the pieces of rabbit into the hot fat to brown on all sides.

5. When the meat is nicely browned, add the sliced onion and brown it slightly.

6. Add the vegetables, broth, and vinegar.

7. Reduce the heat to low, cover the pot, and simmer the stew for 45 minutes or until the meat is done. As the stew is cooking, you can make the dumplings. (See recipe on page 32.)

8. After the stew has simmered for about 45 minutes, spoon the dumplings evenly over the top of the stew. Replace the lid and let the dumplings steam on top of the stew for 15 to 20 minutes. Serve the stew and dumplings hot.

MAKES 6 SERVINGS.

Dumplings

Ma had cooked an especially good supper because they had company. There was stewed jack rabbit with white-flour dumplings and plenty of gravy. —CHAPTER 5

The white-flour dumplings with the rabbit stew made that supper extra special. White flour was more expensive and scarcer on the prairie than the usual whole-wheat flour.

Not only was Ma serving a company dinner, she was also thanking Mr. Edwards for his help with the cabin.

To make dumplings, you will need:

1 cup flour	*2 tablespoons melted shortening*
½ teaspoon salt	*or lard*
1½ teaspoons baking powder	*Mixing bowl*
½ cup milk	*Spoon*

1. Mix the flour, salt, and baking powder in the bowl.
2. Add the milk and melted shortening, and stir just enough to make a soft dough.
3. Spoon the dumplings into the simmering stew as directed in step 8 of Ma's Jackrabbit Stew recipe, page 31.

MAKES 6–8 DUMPLINGS.

Ma's Willow-Bough Broom

They ran back and forth as fast as they could, gathering their skirts full of chips and dumping them in a pile near the fire. But there were still chips on the ground inside the house when Ma began to sweep it with her willow-bough broom. —CHAPTER 6

Before Pa put down the puncheon floor in the little house on the prairie, there was only a dirt floor. Still, Ma wanted the house to be as neat and clean as possible. So she swept the floor with her willow-bough broom, made of slender branches of willow trees tied together around a stout stick for a handle.

To make a willow-bough broom, you will need:

3-foot long stick, about 1 inch to 1½ inches in diameter
Several handfuls of willow branches, each about 2 feet long

2 yards of heavy twine
Heavy-duty scissors

1. Gather the thicker ends of the willow branches evenly around the lower 6 inches of the long stick.
2. Weave the twine in and around the ends of the branches and around the long stick several times to hold them together.

3. Pull the twine as tightly as you can.

4. Tie the ends of the twine together in a firm knot. Cut the ends of the twine close to the knot.

5. Trim the narrow ends of the willow branches so that they are even.

Old Dan Tucker

"Play, Ingalls!" he said. "Play me down the road!"
—CHAPTER 6

As Mr. Edwards began his two-mile walk back home, Pa "played him down the road" with the song "Old Dan Tucker."

The words to "Old Dan Tucker" were written by Daniel Decatur Emmett (also known as Old Dan Emmit) in 1843. The composer of the tune is unknown.

Old— Dan Tuck - er was a fine old man; He washed his face in the

fry - ing pan, He combed his hair with a wag - on wheel, And

died of the tooth - ache in his heel. Git out of the way for

old Dan Tuck - er! He's too late to get his sup - per!

Sup - per's o - ver and the dish - es washed, Noth - ing left but a piece of squash!

$\mathcal{A}$ll day long, every day,

Laura and Mary were busy. When the

dishes were washed and the beds

were made, there was always plenty to

do and to see and to listen to.

—CHAPTER 10

4

Prairie Day

After the Ingallses built the log cabin, their life on the prairie began to settle into a routine. Each day Mary and Laura helped Ma and Pa with chores, but they also had time to play. In the warm months they lay in the tall grass, watching the little prairie chickens and rabbits that lived near the cabin. They explored the prairie, the creeks, and the woods nearby. During the winter months the family spent most of their time inside the cabin. Chores continued as usual, but Laura and Mary's playtime was confined to indoor games.

Life on the prairie did not always follow a routine, however. During the late summer the whole family became very sick with malaria. They suffered for days with chills and fever until Jack, the faithful family bulldog, met Dr. Tan on the prairie and led him to the Ingallses' cabin. Dr. Tan treated them with a bitter-tasting medicine, and soon they began to recover.

The Ingallses dealt with other emergencies too, including a chimney fire in the fall and a bigger fire that raced across the prairie the following spring.

Despite the dangers Laura loved living on the prairie. The family worked hard during the day. At night Pa would sit in the doorway and play his fiddle and sing to Ma and Mary and Laura in the house and to the stars outside.

Frontier Survival

Although days on the prairie usually followed a comfortable routine, there were occasional emergencies. Most people on the prairie did not have a doctor nearby to help them in times of accidents, sickness, or childbirth. Women usually depended on other neighbor women to serve as midwives when babies were born. The Ingallses' neighbor Mrs. Scott helped Caroline Ingalls when Carrie was born in the little prairie house on August 3, 1870.

Many pioneers knew how to treat certain ailments with homemade remedies made with herbs and other natural ingredients. But some illnesses could not be treated, and many pioneers and their children died as a result. In addition, accidents, such as falls or gunshot wounds, often resulted in death.

When the Ingalls family fell ill with malaria, they were very fortunate that Dr. George A. Tann came to help them. Dr. Tann had come to Kansas from Pennsylvania about the same time the Ingallses did to homestead the newly opened land, and he lived about two miles north of the Ingalls cabin. Dr. Tann gave the Ingallses doses of quinine, a powder made from the dried bark of a South American tree. It relieved the symptoms of malaria, caused by a tiny parasite carried by the mosquitoes that bred in the damp creek bottoms near the cabin. For many years quinine was the only known treatment for malaria and one of the few real medicines available to physicians.

Fire was another emergency the Ingallses and other homesteaders faced.

In fact, fires were so common that a pail of water was usually kept on the hearth or by the door in most cabins. Some fires started accidentally by lightning or carelessly tended campfires. Other fires were set by Indian tribes to burn off the dry prairie grasses to make it easier to plant crops and to drive out small animals for hunting. However, sometimes these fires went out of control.

When prairie fires raced across the flat prairie, driven by the winds that blow almost constantly, little could be done to stop them. All pioneers could do was create a firebreak, a wide strip of dirt free of grass or anything else that would burn, that would keep the fire from continuing onto their land. Ideally, settlers plowed a firebreak around their houses and other buildings before it was needed. But sometimes, as in Charles Ingalls's case, they managed to plow one quickly enough to keep the fire away for the moment.

In addition to sickness and fire, pioneers had to deal with other threats to their survival. Drought and insects could ruin crops, wild animals might attack, and outlaws sometimes preyed on settlers.

Fortunately for the Ingalls family, the dire situations that came their way ended without lasting harm, which was not always the case with settlers on the prairie. Laura wrote that Ma often said after they had endured a possible tragedy, "All's well that ends well!"

Ma and Laura's Sun-Dried Blackberries

Every day they brought home pails full of berries, and Ma spread them in the sun to dry. Every day they ate all the blackberries they wanted, and the next winter they would have dried blackberries to stew. —CHAPTER 15

In early July blackberries began to ripen down by the creek, and Ma and Laura went out every afternoon to pick them. The whole family feasted on as many of the fresh berries as they liked, and Ma spread the rest out to dry in the prairie sunshine. Once they were dry, she stored them in covered containers, so the family could eat dried berries throughout the winter.

Today, instead of drying berries, we are more likely to can or freeze them in order to preserve them. But you can dry blackberries if you wish. Dried blackberries (or blueberries or strawberries) can be eaten right from the jar as a snack or added to biscuits or breads. They also can be soaked in water and stewed or made into pies, cobblers, and other tasty treats.

To dry blackberries, you will need:

1 pint fresh blackberries (you can pick them yourself or purchase them)
Medium bowl
Colander or wire sieve
2 tea towels or layers of paper towels and newspapers

Drying rack
Baking pan (large enough for the drying rack to fit inside it)
1 or 2 glass jars
2 pieces of cheesecloth

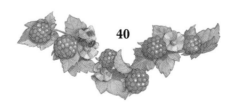

1. Put the berries in a bowl. Take out any berries that are too soft or are damaged in any way. Remove stems, leaves, or other foreign material.

2. Wash the blackberries in cold running water and drain in the colander.

3. Spread the blackberries on one tea towel (or layers of paper towels or clean newspaper) and blot them dry with another tea towel or paper towels.

4. Place the rack in the baking pan and cover the rack with cheesecloth.

5. Spread a layer of blackberries over the cheesecloth and cover them with another piece of cheesecloth.

6. Set the pan of berries in the bright sun for several hours, moving the pan as necessary to keep it in direct sunlight. Shake the pan occasionally to turn the berries for more even drying. If the berries do not dry in one day (and they probably will not), bring them inside for the night and return them to the sunlight the next day. Depending on the amount of sun and the humidity in the air, it may take several days to dry the berries sufficiently.

> Note: Successful berry drying depends on hot, dry conditions. If the berries are not sufficiently dry before you store them, they will mold. If several days of sunshine are not available, place the berries on the rack (minus the cheesecloth) in a warm (120 degrees) oven for several hours.

7. When the berries are thoroughly dry, store them in glass jars with tightly closed lids.

MAKES ABOUT 1 PINT OF DRIED BERRIES.

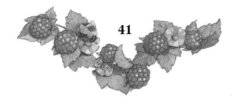

Ma's
Stewed Blackberries

And after all that there were stewed dried blackberries and little cakes. —CHAPTER 19

Later that year, as a special Christmas treat, Ma served some of the dried blackberries she and Laura had picked months before. But she did not serve them dried. Instead, she stewed them by cooking them in some water and sugar so they were soft enough to eat easily.

Ma served little brown sugar cakes with her stewed blackberries on Christmas Day (see recipe on page 76). Stewed blackberries are also good with cookies, spooned over shortcake, or topped with ice cream or whipped cream.

To stew dried blackberries, you will need:

1 cup dried blackberries *Heavy saucepan*
Hot water *Spoon*
4 teaspoons sugar *4 dessert bowls*

1. Put the dried berries in the saucepan. Cover the berries with hot water and let them soak for 10 or 15 minutes.

2. Bring the berries to a simmer over medium heat. Cook them, stirring often, for 20 or 30 minutes or until they are tender.

3. Add the sugar during the last few minutes of cooking and stir to mix.

4. Serve the stewed berries in dessert bowls.

MAKES 4 SERVINGS.

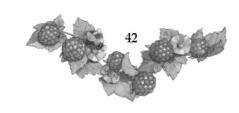

Planting a Prairie Garden

In the daytime everyone was busy. Pa hurried with his plowing, and
Mary and Laura helped Ma plant the early garden seeds. —CHAPTER 25

The arrival of spring on the prairie meant that it was time to plant a garden near the little house. Ma had started sweet potato and cabbage seedlings indoors a few weeks earlier, and they were now ready to set outside. Pa had bought seeds for turnips, carrots, onions, peas, beans, and watermelons in town. Now it was time to plow up the tough prairie sod, plant the seeds, and watch them sprout.

To plant a small prairie garden, you will need:

Vegetable seeds or starter plants
    (among the easiest to grow are
    radishes, lettuce, spinach, carrots,
    peas, and beans)

Garden tools—a spade, a hoe, a rake,
    and a trowel
Fertilizer (optional)
Flat wooden or plastic sticks (optional)
Waterproof pen (optional)

1. Read the directions on the seed envelope or seedling pack to find out the best time of year to plant your vegetables.

2. Select a sunny spot for your garden. If you do not have space for an outdoor garden, you can plant vegetables in a windowbox or a large flowerpot set in a sunny spot.

3. Decide how big your garden will be. Mark the edges with a string, some sticks, or even a few rocks so that you will know just where to dig. You can make your garden square or rectangular.

4. With a spade, turn over the soil in the space you want to plant. Leave narrow strips of grass in place; you will plant your vegetables in the spaces between the strips. Make the soil loose so that the roots of the new plants can grow easily. Mix some fertilizer with the soil if you wish. You can find out from your local garden store which fertilizers are best for your area. Rake the soil smooth.

5. With the hoe or trowel, dig shallow trenches or holes for the seeds or plants. Plant the seeds of each kind of plant in a row or section by itself. The seed envelope or seedling pack will tell you how far apart and how deep to plant the seeds. Cover the seeds lightly with soil, using the hoe or rake. Tap the soil down gently on top of the seeds.

6. If you are planting seedlings, use the trowel to make a small hole in the dirt for each plant and set the plant in the hole. Fill the hole with soil and gently press the soil around the plant to hold it firmly in place. If you wish, write the names of the vegetables you have planted on some flat wooden or plastic sticks with waterproof ink and stick them in the soil next to the plantings.

7. When you have finished planting, water the garden gently with a watering can or sprinkler so the seeds will not wash away and the seedlings will not fall over. Water just enough to dampen the soil. Water your garden often, especially if there is no rain. As the plants get larger and stronger, you will need to water them more thoroughly.

8. In a few weeks after planting, you can begin to harvest some of your early crops, such as radishes, lettuce, and spinach. It will not be much longer until the other vegetables are ready.

Ma's Sweet Potato Plants

One evening Pa came from the field before sunset and he helped Ma
set out the cabbage plants and the sweet-potato plants. . . . Ma had saved one of
the Christmas sweet potatoes, and planted it in a box. The sweet potato had sent
up a stem and green leaves from every one of its eyes. —CHAPTER 25

Ma had grown a sweet potato all through the winter. She probably packed the potato in dry sand and kept it in a corner of the cabin until early spring. Then she planted it in a pot of soil, watered it, and let it grow.

You can start growing sweet potato plants anytime for your windowsill garden, but if you are going to plant them outside, it is best to start them in late winter or early spring.

To grow a sweet potato plant, you will need:

1 sweet potato	*Water*
Sharp knife	*Shallow pot or box*
Cutting board	*Potting soil*
2 saucers	

1. Cut the sweet potato in half crosswise on a cutting board. Put each half, cut side down, in a saucer. Add water to each saucer until the water comes about a ½ inch up the sides of the potato.

2. Place the potatoes near a sunny window and check the water level in the saucers every day. Add water when needed so that the water remains at the ½ inch spot on the potatoes. In a few days little sprouts will start to grow from the eyes of the potatoes. (Potato eyes are little dimples scattered over the surface of the potato.)

3. When the sprouts are about 2 inches long, plant the potatoes in pots of soil.

You can plant each half of the potato as it is already growing. Or you can carefully cut the potato halves into pieces that each have one sprout growing from it, and plant each piece individually.

4. To plant the potato pieces, fill the shallow pot or box half full of potting soil. Place halves or pieces of sprouted sweet potatoes in the soil and press them in gently. Pour more potting soil around the potato pieces so that just the sprouts are sticking up above the soil.

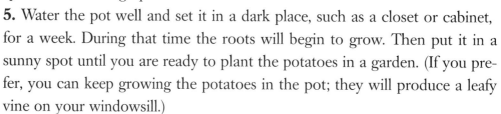

5. Water the pot well and set it in a dark place, such as a closet or cabinet, for a week. During that time the roots will begin to grow. Then put it in a sunny spot until you are ready to plant the potatoes in a garden. (If you prefer, you can keep growing the potatoes in the pot; they will produce a leafy vine on your windowsill.)

6. In the spring, when the soil is warm, you can plant the potatoes outside. Dig a hole in the ground for each potato plant. Carefully remove the plant from the soil in the pot. Put the plant into the hole so that the green stems are above the ground. Fill the hole around the plant with soil and press it in firmly. Water each plant well. Continue to water the sweet potato plants during the summer months.

7. When the leaves begin to turn yellow and dry in the fall, carefully dig down into the earth and pull up a handful of sweet potatoes from each plant. Wash the sweet potatoes, dry them thoroughly, and store them in a cool, dark place until you are ready to cook them. (See page 74 for the recipe for Mr. Edwards's Christmas Sweet Potatoes.)

By Lo, Baby Bunting

Ma built up the fire and drew her rocker near it, and she sat rocking
*Baby Carrie and singing softly to her, "By lo, baby bunting." —*CHAPTER 16

Since Pa spent many days hunting, this song was probably especially meaningful to Ma as she sang it to Baby Carrie. This lullaby is based on a Mother Goose rhyme and has been sung to babies for hundreds of years. "Baby bunting" was a nickname for any infant wrapped in "bunting," an old-fashioned name for a soft blanket.

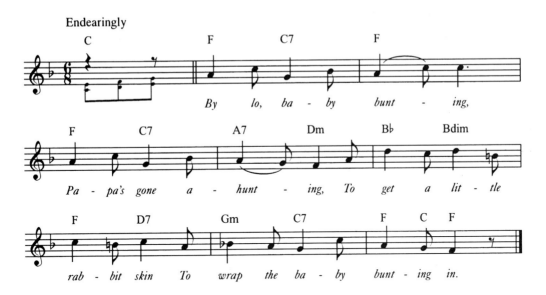

By lo, ba - by bunt - ing, Pa - pa's gone a - hunt - ing, To get a lit - tle rab - bit skin To wrap the ba - by bunt - ing in.

47

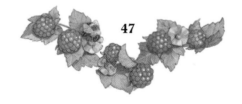

$\mathcal{S}$uddenly a dozen long-horned

cattle burst out of the prairie, not far

from the stable. . . . Their tails stood up

and their fierce horns tossed

and their feet pounded the ground.

—CHAPTER 13

5

Prairie Animals

*P*a wanted to move to the prairie to be where people had not yet crowded out the wildlife. On the prairie Mary and Laura noticed all the birds that flew across the wide sky and the animals that ran through the tall grass. One day they even made a game of chasing some little velvety-brown gophers.

There were larger, fiercer animals, too. Occasionally some of them came too close to the little house. One night a pack of big wolves circled the house. Pa had not yet made the door for the cabin and had covered the opening with one of Ma's quilts. The wolves howled and paced, but Pa and Jack guarded the doorway. Finally, the wolves moved on, leaving only their tracks around the house and stable. Another night a terrible scream woke the family in the middle of the night. It turned out to be a panther, leaping through the tops of the trees near the creek.

Not all the animals Laura saw on the prairie were wild. One day a large herd of Texas longhorn cattle passed close to the little house. The two cowboys driving the herd asked Pa to help them keep the cattle from falling down into the ravines near the creek. It was hot, dusty work, but at the end of it Pa brought home some fresh beef along with a cow and her calf. The cow meant the family would have milk and butter for as long as they stayed in the little house on the prairie.

Wild and Domestic Prairie Animals

O ne of the main attractions of prairie living was the abundance of wild animals. Settlers like Charles Ingalls had no trouble bringing home fresh game for the family to eat; the prairie was teeming with jackrabbits, prairie hens, deer, and wild turkeys. Settlers also hunted and trapped animals for their furs, including red foxes, glossy brown beavers, muskrats, silky-furred minks, and wolves with thick, shaggy pelts.

Although animals on the prairie were plentiful, in Laura's time there were already signs that people were taking advantage of the seemingly endless supply. Millions of buffalo had once roamed the plains from northern Canada all the way down to southern Texas, and tribes of Plains Indians had depended on them for food as well as clothing and shelter. However, over several decades, white men had hunted them for sport and commercial purposes, and by Laura's time their numbers were significantly reduced. (By 1900 the buffalo would be nearly extinct.) This, in turn, caused a crisis for the Indians, who had to adapt quickly to other ways of life in order to survive.

In addition to the wild animals of the prairie, settlers kept domesticated animals, and the Ingallses' animals were typical for a frontier family. Most homesteaders had a watchdog like Jack to protect the family from wild animals and strangers. Horses like Pet and Patty, the two black mustangs, pulled covered wagons across the prairie and later helped plow the thick prairie sod. Cows and pigs were rare on the claims of the new settlers, although occasionally a settler would be able to obtain them, the way Charles Ingalls acquired a cow and her calf as payment for herding cattle in one of the legendary Old West cattle drives.

The cattle drive that Pa helped with was one of many that passed over the prairie. Cowboys led great herds of cattle for miles, from southern Texas up through Kansas to the major railroad loading stations at Abilene and Kansas City. There were three major cattle trails: the Western, the Chisholm, and the Shawnee. The eastern fork of the Shawnee Trail ran quite close to the Ingallses' farm in southern Kansas. It is likely that the herd of cattle Pa helped manage was following this trail north to the railroad yards of Kansas City.

For little girls like Mary and Laura the animals on the prairie were wondrous things, whether they were wild or not. But for grown-ups like Pa and Ma the wildlife of the prairie meant food for their families and furs to trade for things they could not make or grow for themselves. As Laura wrote, the abundance of wildlife caused Pa to shout for joy: "I tell you, Caroline, there's everything we want here. We can live like kings!"

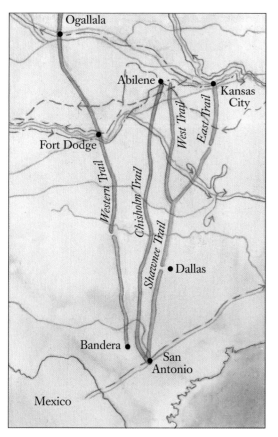

The three major cattle trails.

Prairie Corn Bread

And everyone was happy because now there would be milk to drink, and perhaps even butter for the cornbread. —CHAPTER 13

One of the big barrels in every pioneer's covered wagon contained cornmeal, which was the basis for all kinds of breads—johnnycake, hoecake, corn cakes, corn dodgers, hush puppies, and, perhaps most popular of all, corn bread.

To make corn bread, you will need:

2 tablespoons shortening or lard	*2 cups buttermilk*
3 eggs	*9-inch skillet or cake pan*
2 cups cornmeal	*Large bowl*
1 teaspoon baking soda	*Mixing fork*
1 teaspoon salt	

1. Preheat the oven to 375 degrees. Put the shortening in the pan and set the pan in the warm oven to melt the shortening and heat the pan.

2. Put the eggs into the large bowl. Beat them with the fork until thick and foamy. Add the cornmeal, baking soda, and salt to the eggs. Mix well. Add the buttermilk to the batter and mix.

3. Remove the pan from the oven and pour the melted shortening into the batter. Stir. Spoon the batter into the hot pan (or shape it into two half circles as Ma did) and put the pan back in the oven.

4. Bake the corn bread for about 25 minutes or until golden brown on top. Cut into wedges and serve hot with plenty of butter.

MAKES 6 SERVINGS.

Pa's Animal Book

"This country's cram-jammed with game," Pa told Laura.
"I saw fifty deer if I saw one, and antelope, squirrels, rabbits, birds of all kinds.
*The creek's full of fish." —*CHAPTER 4

Perhaps Laura's fascination with animals began in the little house in the Big Woods, where she read Pa's "big green animal book," which was actually called *The Wonders of the Animal World* by G. Hartwig. Pa's book had pictures of lions, tigers, polar bears, and other exotic animals.

Mary and Laura may have made their own animal book with drawings of animals they saw near their little house. Paper for such projects was rare in their cabin on the Kansas prairie, but Ma may have smoothed out some of the brown wrapping paper she always saved from Pa's purchases in town for them to use.

To make your own animal book, you will need:

Brown wrapping paper or brown paper bags	*18-inch piece of string or twine*
Scissors	*Reference books about animals*
Ruler	*Old magazines (optional)*
Hole punch	*Pencil*
	Glue (optional)

1. Cut the brown paper into five or six 8½-×-11-inch sheets.
2. Stack the sheets of paper evenly and fold the stack of paper in half.
3. Use the hole punch to make a hole ½ inch in from the folded edge of the paper, 2 inches down from the top.

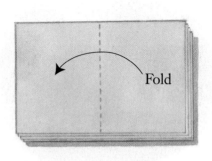

Fold

Make a second hole ½ inch in from the folded edge and 2 inches up from the bottom. (It may be easier to punch holes in one or two sheets of paper at a time rather than try to punch through the whole stack at once.)

4. Thread the string or twine through the holes and tie it in a bow on the front of the book to hold the pages together. (You can add more pages later as you need them.)

5. Look in reference books and/or old magazines for pictures of animals that you want to record in your book.

6. Use the pencil to sketch them on the pages of your book, or cut out pictures from old magazines and glue them in.

7. Find as much information as you can about each animal and write it in your book near the animal's picture. You can even find out what each animal's footprint looks like and sketch it in.

When you are out walking, watch for real birds and other animals and make notes about them in your animal book.

Cowboy Bandannas

They wore flaps of leather over their legs, and spurs, and wide-brimmed hats.
Handkerchiefs were knotted around their necks, and pistols were on their hips.
—CHAPTER 13

The cowboys Pa met were dressed in chaps (leather flaps worn over their pants for protection from the sharp cattle horns), boots with spurs, and hats with wide brims to keep the sun off their faces. They wore handkerchiefs called bandannas tied around their necks.

Cowboys and pioneer men alike found bandannas useful for many things. They wore bandannas around their necks or foreheads to keep sweat from trickling down their shirts or into their eyes. When the dust from the trail was blowing, they folded their bandannas into large triangles and tied them over their noses and mouths to filter the air they breathed. They used the bandannas as handkerchiefs, washcloths, fly swatters, carrying cases, and even sandwich wrappers. In emergencies bandannas served as bandages or slings or tourniquets.

To fold your own cowboy bandanna, you will need:

A bandanna, or any 18-inch square piece of red or
blue cotton cloth

To make a dust mask:

1. Lay your bandanna down on a flat surface and fold one corner to the opposite corner as shown.

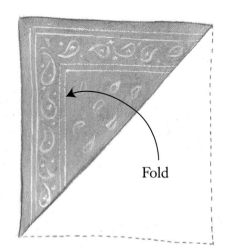

Fold

2. Hold two corners together at the back of your head. Pull the front of the bandanna up over your nose to cover your nose and mouth.

3. Tie the two corners together behind your head.

3. Tie the two corners together in front for a neckerchief.

To make a neckerchief:

1. Repeat step 1 above.

2. From the folded edge of the bandanna, fold over a section about 2 inches wide as shown. Continue to fold over the same amount until you have a narrow scarf.

PRAIRIE SONGS

I Ride an Old Paint

Laura stood in her nightgown at the window. . . .
"Is that singing Pa?" she asked.
"Yes," Pa said.
"The cowboys are singing the cattle to sleep."—CHAPTER 13

Since sudden, loud noises might cause the huge herd to stampede, cowboys sang softly to the cattle as they drove them along the trail.

This is one of the most popular songs from the days of the cowboy on the cattle trail.

Slowly, with rocking motion

I ride an old paint— and I lead an old dan,— I'm off to Mon - tan - a for to throw the hoo - li - han._____ They feed in the cou - lees, they wa - ter in the draw, Their tails are all mat - ted and their backs are all raw.

$\mathcal{B}$efore dawn, Pa went away.
When Laura and Mary woke, he was gone

and everything was empty and lonely. It was

not as though Pa had only gone hunting.

He was going to town, and he would not

be back for four long days.

—CHAPTER 17

6

Pa Goes to Town

After the little log house was finished and before winter set in, Pa decided it was time to make a trip to town. The family needed some supplies, and Ma wanted to send a letter back to Wisconsin.

Laura and Mary waited for four long days for Pa to return, and on the fourth night they woke to find him standing by the fire. He was nearly frozen, but he hugged the girls, wrapping both of them in Ma's big woolen shawl. When he had warmed up a bit, he showed them what he had bought in town—nails, cornmeal, fat pork, salt, a little sack of white sugar, and eight small glass panes for windows.

When winter was over, Pa made another trip to Independence to sell his furs and buy a plow and some seeds. After five days he came into the house with his arms full of bundles. He dropped sacks of brown sugar, white flour, cornmeal, salt, and coffee on the table along with seeds and seed potatoes. Pa had even managed to buy a few surprises for Ma and the girls. There were a length of pretty calico for Ma and combs for Mary and Laura to wear in their hair.

Pa's trips to town meant long days of watching and waiting, but when he was safely home, Laura felt comfortable again. "Everything was all right when Pa was there."

Independence

When the Ingalls family first settled on the Kansas prairie, the closest town, Independence, was only a few weeks old. Five settlers from the nearby town of Oswego had come out to the area on August 21, 1869, camping out on land that would later become the city of Independence and the county seat of Montgomery County, Kansas.

The United States government hadn't finalized its treaties with the Osage tribe for the land, but these settlers didn't wait. They made their own treaties, paying the Osage chief fifty dollars for an area covering about twenty-five square miles. Almost immediately, they brought in logs and built a two-story hotel called the Judson House.

Soon a few more small houses began to appear. Since there was no sawmill yet in Independence, most of the first houses were built quickly from

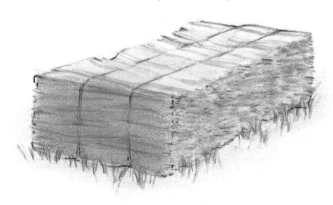

bundles of hay, giving the town its nickname, Haytown. The houses were said to be quite comfortable; some even had real doors, a window or two, and stoves.

Around the first of October a store was put up—Wilson E. Irwin Groceries. It was furnished with goods brought in by wagon from the nearest railroad stop in Miami County, about ninety miles away. It is likely that Charles Ingalls bought some of his supplies there when he made his first trip to town.

By December three sawmills were operating in Independence. Within six weeks after the first lumber was turned out, forty buildings had been erected. The first issue of the *Independence Pioneer*, the town's first newspaper, came out in late November. More stores opened, and a one-room schoolhouse was built.

It was not easy to send or receive mail in Independence in the first few months. Mail carriers had to ride on horseback to Oswego, about thirty miles away, to collect letters and parcels for people in Independence. By July of 1870 the town had arranged for a stagecoach to come in from Oswego with passengers and mail.

Before Independence was a year old, over four hundred people were living there, according to the 1870 census. Within another year, a thousand more had moved in.

The Ingallses left the area in 1871, but Independence continued to grow and thrive. Today it is a prosperous community with a population of about ten thousand people. The plot of land that Charles Ingalls first farmed is now a small cattle ranch, and a replica of the Ingalls cabin has been built near the original site of the little house on the prairie.

Pa's Homecoming Fried Salt Pork

Everything was all right when Pa was there. And now he had nails, and cornmeal, and fat pork, and salt, and everything. He would not have to go to town again for a long time. —CHAPTER 17

Fried salt pork was a favorite food of the pioneers. It is similar to the bacon we buy today, but is mostly fat with just a few lean streaks. Some people call it streak-o'-lean or fatback.

Chunks of salt pork are often boiled with vegetables such as green beans or turnip greens to give them extra flavor. Slices of salt pork can be fried and served as a salty, crunchy main course.

To make fried salt pork, you will need:

1 pound salt pork	*Large skillet*
1 teaspoon pepper	*Cooking fork or tongs*
1 cup flour	*Platter*
Sharp knife	*Aluminum foil*
Cutting board	

1. Rinse the salt pork in cold water. Use the sharp knife to trim off the rind, if any, on the cutting board.

2. Slice the pork into slices about ¼ inch thick. (If you do not want the slices to be too crunchy, you can simmer them in barely boiling water for about 5 minutes. Drain and pat the slices dry on a paper towel before you begin step 3.)

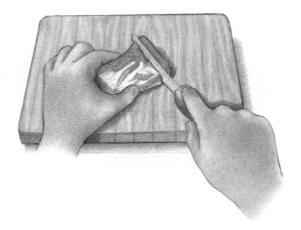

3. Sprinkle pepper and flour liberally over the tops of the slices, turn the slices over, and sprinkle more pepper and flour on the other sides of the slices.

4. Place the slices of pork in a single layer in the cold skillet. Set the skillet over medium-low heat and cook the slices slowly until most of the fat has cooked out. (When the fat has cooked out, the slices will shrink and be limp.)

5. Turn the heat to medium high, and cook the slices about 3 minutes on each side until they are a light golden brown.

6. Remove the slices of salt pork to a platter, cover them with foil, and place in a warm oven until you are ready to serve them. Save the skillet with the pork fat in it to make cream gravy (see recipe for Salt Pork Cream Gravy on page 64) if desired.

MAKES 4 SERVINGS.

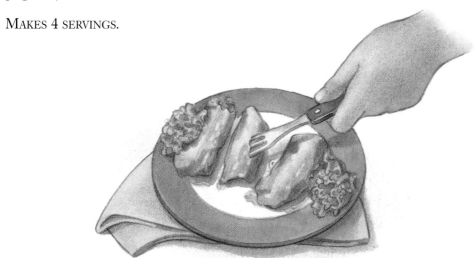

Salt Pork Cream Gravy

That was the happiest supper they had had for a long time. Pa was safely home again. The fried salt pork was very good, after so many months of eating ducks and geese and turkeys and venison. And nothing had ever tasted so good as those crackers and the little green sour pickles. —CHAPTER 21

After the slices of salt pork are cooked and removed from the skillet, you can make a delicious thick gravy to pour over them. Serve crackers, such as saltines or any other plain crackers, with the salt pork and gravy to have the same meal the Ingallses had the night Pa came home from town.

To make salt pork cream gravy, you will need:

Fat left from the cooked salt pork
2 teaspoons flour
1 cup cream
Pepper

The skillet you used to cook the salt pork
Heatproof cup or jar
Wooden spoon

1. Carefully pour most of the fat left in the skillet (all but about 2 tablespoons, or just enough to cover the bottom of the skillet) into a heatproof cup or jar. (You can use the extra fat later or just discard it after it cools.)

2. Set the skillet on medium heat and sprinkle 2 teaspoons of flour into the skillet.

3. Stir the flour into the fat with the wooden spoon. Keep stirring until the flour begins to turn a light brown.

4. Slowly pour in the cream and heat it to the boiling point, stirring constantly.

5. When the mixture thickens, it is ready to serve. Season it with a pinch of black pepper, if you wish. You can pour the gravy over the slices on the platter or serve it separately from a bowl.

Mary and Laura's Star Headbands

The combs were made of black rubber . . . with curving slits cut in it, and in the very middle of it a little five-pointed star was cut out. —CHAPTER 21

Pa found something special for Mary and Laura on his second trip to Independence. He brought them black rubber combs (we call them headbands today) with designs cut out so that the brightly colored ribbons underneath showed through. Mary's ribbon was blue and Laura's was red.

Although Mary's and Laura's headbands were store-bought and made of rubber, you can easily make similar ones for yourself and your friends with felt and ribbon.

Use any color ribbon you like for your headband. You can even change the color of the ribbon to match your outfit.

To make your headband, you will need:

> *Strip of black felt, 1 inch wide by 12 inches long*
> *Red or blue ribbon, ³/₄ inch wide by 36 inches long*
> *Scissors*
> *Ruler*

1. Cut a ³/₄-inch vertical slit ¹/₂ inch in from each end of the felt strip.
2. Cut a star shape in the center of the felt strip as shown. Cut some "curving slits" on either side of the star down the length of the headband.

3. Insert one end of the ribbon through one of the slits at the end of the felt strip. Run the ribbon under the headband and pull the ribbon up through the slit at the other end.

4. Adjust the ribbon so that the ends are the same length.

5. Place the headband across the top of your hair so that the star is in the center of your head.

6. Tie the ends of the ribbon under your hair at the back of your neck.

7. Trim the ends of the ribbon if they are too long.

Ma's Warm and Cozy Shawl

Pa wrapped Laura in Ma's big shawl, and then he hugged her. . . .
The shawl was so large that Mary wrapped the other end of it around her. . . .
Pa sat on the bench and he took Mary on one knee and Laura on the other
and he hugged them against him, all snuggled in the shawl. —CHAPTER 17

Like most of the other women pioneering on the prairie, Ma had a large shawl that she could wear for many purposes. Ma probably made her shawl of soft woolen cloth. Shawls also were sometimes knitted or crocheted with yarn.

To make a warm and cozy shawl like Ma's, you will need:

1 square (54 inches × 54 inches) of soft woolen fabric
(purchase this at a fabric store)
Scissors

1. Use the scissors to carefully trim the selvages (woven edges) off of the fabric.
2. Pull out threads from each edge of the fabric until you have an inch of fringe all the way around. Tie the threads at the corners to keep the edges from unraveling further.
3. Fold the piece of fabric in half diagonally. Place the folded edge around your shoulders with the side points of the shawl over your arms and the middle point in the back. The fringed edges will make a pretty decoration along the bottom edges of the shawl. You can also open the shawl to use as a small blanket.

Green Grows the Laurel

*When Laura and Mary were in bed Pa took down his fiddle. Softly he played and softly sang, "So green grows the laurel, and so does the rue, So woeful, my love, at the parting with you." —*CHAPTER 16

This is an old song that originated in England. Its verses tell of a soldier going to war after his sweetheart falls in love with another man. But Pa did not sing the verses before he left on his long trip to town; he only sang the chorus. It was his way of letting Ma know that he would miss her.

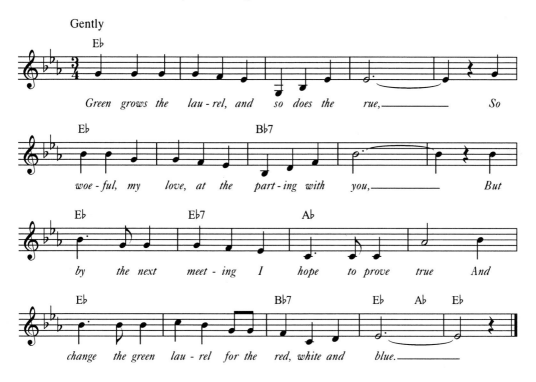

Gently

Green grows the lau-rel, and so does the rue,_____ So

woe-ful, my love, at the part-ing with you,_____ But

by the next meet-ing I hope to prove true And

change the green lau-rel for the red, white and blue._____

69

$\mathcal{M}$r. Edwards said that Santa Claus
knew everybody. And he had recognized Santa
at once by his whiskers. Santa Claus had
the longest, thickest, whitest set of whiskers
west of the Mississippi.

—Chapter 19

7

Christmas on the Prairie

As Christmas on the prairie approached, the cold, short days of winter kept Laura and Mary inside, stitching quilt blocks and playing with their paper dolls. But they were worried. There was no snow on the ground, and it had been raining hard for days. They didn't know if Santa Claus could get there with no snow for the sleigh or if he'd be able to cross the swollen creek. Two very unhappy little girls crawled under their patchwork quilts on Christmas Eve.

But in the morning they awoke to a big surprise. Mr. Edwards was there, and he had seen Santa Claus! He had even brought presents from Santa to Mary and Laura. While Ma put the presents in the stockings she had hung up on the mantelshelf, Mr. Edwards told them all about his visit with Santa Claus, right on the main street of Independence.

Soon, though, Ma said, "You may look now, girls." And Mary and Laura ran to look in their stockings. The first thing Laura saw was a brand-new tin cup. Next she pulled out a long stick of peppermint candy. A little heart-shaped cake, sparkling with grains of white sugar across the top, was wrapped up and nestled down in the stocking, and in the toe of each stocking was a shiny new penny.

"Oh, thank you, Mr. Edwards! Thank you!" Mary and Laura said. It was a happy Christmas, after all.

Christmas Traditions

Many of the customs that are part of American Christmas celebrations today began to be popular about the time Laura and Mary Ingalls were little girls. Before then Christmas in the United States had been celebrated very simply. Some people hardly acknowledged it at all, even as a religious holiday. Others marked it with a few gifts and decorations and a special dinner.

On Christmas Eve in *Little House on the Prairie*, Ma hung the stockings by the fireplace, even though there was little hope that Santa Claus could get to the cabin that night.

Hanging up Christmas stockings on Christmas Eve came from the Dutch tradition of placing wooden shoes near the fireplace for St. Nicholas to fill with small gifts. St. Nicholas was a generous man who lived in the fourth century. Nearly fifty years before the Ingallses celebrated Christmas in the little house on the prairie, Clement Clarke Moore had written his famous poem, "A Visit from St. Nicholas." The wide publication of this poem made popular the idea of St. Nicholas filling stockings in every household. Moore was also one of the first to give St. Nicholas reindeer to pull his sleigh. By the time Mary and Laura were little girls, the image of Santa and his reindeer was very common.

The Christmas tree, so much a

part of Christmas celebrations today, was slower to become a tradition. Laura did not see or even know about a Christmas tree until she was nearly eight years old and saw a decorated tree in the church in Walnut Grove.

The Germans had decorated evergreen trees for Christmas for several hundred years, but it was not until early in the nineteenth century that the custom spread to America. Most of the Christmas trees then were small, tabletop-size trees and were mostly in the homes of wealthier people in northeastern cities. However, as the custom began to spread, churches and community halls began to decorate larger trees as part of the Christmas season.

Although thirty-one states had officially recognized Christmas as a legal holiday by 1865, it was not until June 1870 that the United States Congress voted to make it a national holiday. That was the year after the Ingallses built their cabin on the prairie.

Mr. Edwards's Christmas Sweet Potatoes

Ma gasped. Mr. Edwards was taking sweet potatoes out of his pockets. . . . He thought
Ma and Pa might like them with the Christmas turkey. There were nine sweet potatoes.
Mr. Edwards had brought them all the way from town, too. It was just too much.
—CHAPTER 19

Mr. Edwards brought nine sweet potatoes with him on Christmas Day. Ma baked all but one in the fireplace coals; she saved one to plant in her garden the next spring.

You can bake sweet potatoes too, but unlike Ma you can use an oven or even a microwave (see the microwave instructions at the end of the recipe).

To bake sweet potatoes, you will need:

1 sweet potato per person	*A fork or skewer*
Shortening or oil	*Serving plate*
Salt and pepper (optional)	*Thick cloth*
Brown sugar and cinnamon	*Table knife*
(optional)	

1. Preheat the oven to 375 degrees.

2. Scrub the sweet potatoes clean under running water, then rub a little shortening or oil all over each potato to keep the skin from drying out.

3. Prick each sweet potato with the fork or skewer several times. This allows steam to escape during baking; otherwise the potatoes may split or even explode.

4. Set the potatoes on the middle rack of the oven.

5. Bake the potatoes for 1 hour or until they are soft enough to yield when you squeeze them slightly. Carefully remove the potatoes from the oven and place them on a serving plate.

6. Cut an X in the top of each

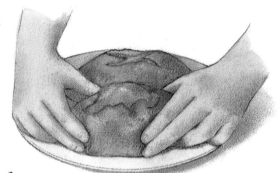

potato and gently squeeze the sides so that the meat inside puffs up a little bit in the center.

7. Serve the potatoes immediately, or cover them with a thick cloth to keep them warm until you're ready to eat them. Serve the sweet potatoes with butter and either salt and pepper or a sprinkling of brown sugar and cinnamon.

Microwave instructions: To microwave sweet potatoes, follow steps 2–3, then arrange the potatoes in a circle on a paper towel in the microwave. Cook them on High for 5 minutes. Turn them over and cook them for 5 minutes more. Squeeze the potatoes slightly to see if they are soft. If they are not soft, continue turning and baking them for 1 minute at a time until they are done.

Ma's Brown Sugar Christmas Cakes

*These little cakes were made with brown sugar and they
did not have white sugar sprinkled over their tops.* —CHAPTER 19

White sugar was a very rare treat for the pioneers, and they used it sparingly when they had any. The first time Pa made a trip to Independence, he brought back "a little paper sack full of pure white sugar." Ma allowed Mary and Laura to have a taste of it, but then she put it away to save for a special occasion.

The little heart-shaped cakes that Mary and Laura found in their Christmas stockings were extra special because they were made with white sugar and white flour. The cakes that Ma made for Christmas dinner that afternoon were made with brown sugar.

To make brown sugar cakes to have with stewed dried blackberries (see recipe for Ma's Stewed Blackberries on page 42) or other fruit, you will need:

shortening for greasing cookie sheet	*Cookie sheet*
1¾ cup all-purpose flour	*Mixing bowl*
2½ teaspoons baking powder	*Wooden spoon*
¼ teaspoon salt	*Table knife*
½ cup firmly packed brown sugar	*Fork*
¼ cup (4 tablespoons) cold butter	*Tablespoon*
¾ cup milk	*Wire rack*

1. Preheat oven to 450 degrees. Lightly grease the cookie sheet.
2. Mix together the flour, baking powder, salt, and sugar in the mixing bowl with the spoon.

3. Use the table knife to cut the butter into small pieces. Add it to the dry ingredients in the bowl.

4. With the fork (or your fingers), blend the butter into the flour mixture until it is crumbly.

5. Stir the milk into the flour mixture with the fork, just until it is blended in well.

6. Use the tablespoon to drop egg-size portions of dough onto the cookie sheet, about 3 inches apart.

7. Bake the cakes for 10–12 minutes or until they are lightly browned.

8. Remove the cakes from the oven and slide them from the cookie sheet to the rack to cool. Serve them warm or at room temperature, with butter and jam or with berries or other fruit and whipped cream.

MAKES 8 CAKES.

Mary and Laura's Christmas Paper Dolls

Mary and Laura stayed close by the fire, sewing their nine-patch quilt blocks, or cutting paper dolls from scraps of wrapping-paper, and hearing the wet sound of the rain.
—CHAPTER 19

Mary and Laura did not have many things to play with in their cabin on the prairie. To pass the cold, dreary days of winter, they made their own games and toys after they helped Ma with the household chores of the day.

One of their favorite pastimes was playing with paper dolls. They made dolls and outfits from bits of wrapping paper that Ma saved, probably the plain brown paper from the parcels Pa had brought from Independence.

You can make your own paper dolls, too, from wrapping paper left over from birthdays and holidays. Keep the paper dolls and their clothes in an envelope or a box so that they will be ready to play with again on the next rainy day.

For each paper doll, you will need:

1 piece of brown or white wrapping paper, about 8 × 5 inches
Pencil or pen
Colored pens or crayons (optional)
Scissors

1. On the wrapping paper, draw a simple outline of a doll as shown.

2. Draw a face and hair on the head of the doll with a black pen or colored pens.

3. Cut out the doll with the scissors.

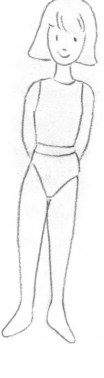

For paper doll clothes, you will need:

Scraps of brown, white, or colored paper,
gift wrap, tissue paper, etc.
Pencil
Colored pens or crayons (optional)
Ribbons, buttons, and
other trim (optional)
Glue (optional)
Scissors

1. Use the paper doll you made in the first part of the activity as a pattern for the clothes.

2. Lay the doll on a piece of paper and trace its outline onto the paper. Remove the doll from the paper and set it aside.

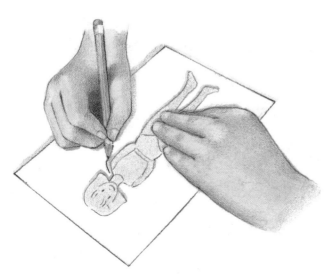

3. Decide where you want the neckline, sleeve cuffs, and hemlines of a shirt, skirt, dress, or pants to be. Mark these on the paper.

4. Sketch the sleeves and skirts around the outline in the style you prefer. Draw tabs in several places as shown on the next page. These tabs will help hold the clothes on the doll.

5. Decorate the clothes with colored pens or crayons, or glue on bits of other paper and trim if you wish.

6. Cut out the clothes, following the outlines. Don't forget to cut out the tabs, too! Put the clothes on the doll by folding the tabs around the back.

7. Repeat the activity to make as many clothes for your paper dolls as you wish.

Jingle Bells

It did not seem at all like Christmas time.
Pa and Ma sat silent by the fire. After a while Ma asked why Pa
didn't play the fiddle, and he said, "I don't seem to have the
*heart to, Caroline." —*CHAPTER 19

If Pa had felt like playing the fiddle, "Jingle Bells" is likely one of the songs he would have chosen.

Originally titled "The One Horse Open Sleigh," this has been a popular holiday song since it was introduced in 1857. The words and music were written by James Pierpont. Today we usually sing the chorus to a slightly different tune from the one that Mr. Pierpont wrote. This is the original version and is probably the one Pa learned and played on his fiddle.

"So you've seen Indians at last,
have you, Laura? I noticed they have a
camp in a little valley west of here."

—CHAPTER 11

8

Indian Camp

Laura's first glimpse of her Indian neighbors was a surprise. Pa had gone hunting, and two young men from the nearby camp came to the cabin. The men wore leather moccasins, and skunk skins hung from leather thongs around their waists.

By midsummer the Indians had left their camp behind, so Pa took Mary and Laura to see it. In the fall the Indians returned to their camp, and one of their leaders stopped by to visit. He and Pa sat by the fire, ate their dinner together, and smoked their pipes, all in silence. Pa felt that he and the Indian had formed a friendship.

Not all the Indians in the area were friendly, however. Many were unhappy that the Ingallses and the other settlers had moved into their territory. That spring the Indians gathered to decide what to do. The leader who was Pa's friend, Soldat du Chêne, talked the other Indians out of waging war against the white settlers who had come onto their land. Hundreds of Indians filed past the cabin on their way south to their new homes.

Pa soon learned, though, that he and the other settlers also had to leave. The book ends as it begins, with Ma, Pa, Laura, Mary, and Carrie in the covered wagon, traveling across the wide-open prairie.

The Osage

The Osage were part of the greater family of Plains Indians who lived in various parts of North America. They originally lived in the vast area that is now Missouri and Arkansas, but as settlers began to move in, the Osage were pressed farther west.

As the Osage moved west, they were no longer able to farm the land as they once had. By the time Laura encountered them, they had become buffalo hunters and followed the herds over the prairies. They lived in tipis made of buffalo skins stretched over long poles, which were easy to take apart, move, and set up again. They usually set up camp near rivers or streams so that they would be close to fresh water.

Like other prairie tribes, the Osage relied on the buffalo for many things. Buffalo meat was a staple of their diet, and they also used the skin for clothing and tents and made tools from the sinews and bones. The Osage were careful to kill only enough buffalo to supply their needs so that the rest of the herd was free to keep multiplying. However, once the

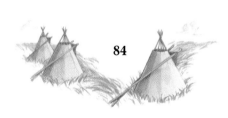

settlers began to hunt the buffalo, the numbers of buffalo quickly began to dwindle, which dramatically endangered the Osage way of life.

In 1868, the year the Ingallses moved from the Big Woods to Chariton County, Missouri, the Osage signed a treaty with the United States government. They agreed to sell a strip of their land in Kansas called the Diminished Reserve to the United States for eighteen cents an acre. When Charles Ingalls heard that news, he decided to move his family to the brand-new territory as soon as it opened to settlers. However, the United States government never actually paid the Osage for the land. While the Ingallses were living on the prairie, many of the Osage were angry that the Ingallses and other settlers were living on the strip of land that was still in dispute and that they felt still belonged to them.

Although many of the Osage wanted to wage war against the settlers, their chief, Soldat du Chêne, was able to convince them not to fight, and instead they moved south into Oklahoma Territory.

The land dispute was finally settled in 1872, when the Osage agreed to give up their land in Kansas and moved to reservation lands in Oklahoma. Today the Osage own land individually, and the discovery of oil on their reservation has made them wealthy. In 1990 there were over 9,500 Osage living in the United States.

Pemmican

Then Pa picked up a smoke-blackened forked stick.
And he said that the pot had hung from a stick laid across
the top of two upright, forked sticks. —CHAPTER 14

The Osage hunted jackrabbits and other wild game and made stew much as Ma did (see Ma's Jackrabbit Stew recipe, page 30), cooked in a pot hanging over a fire. They also dried meats for their hunting journeys and for winter, when they knew food would be scarce.

Pemmican was a staple food for many Indian tribes, including the Osage. Strips of dried buffalo or venison (deer meat) were pounded into a paste, then mixed with fat and, sometimes, with parched corn and dried berries. Pemmican was nutritious and easy to store and carry.

To make one version of pemmican, you will need:

2 ounces beef jerky (available at grocery stores)

2 tablespoons lard or shortening

2 tablespoons cornmeal

½ cup raisins (or other dried fruits such as apples, plums, blackberries, cranberries, etc.)

Mortar and pestle (or heavy bowl and wooden spoon)

Mixing bowl

Wooden spoon

Sharp knife

Cutting board

Wire rack

Plastic wrap

1. Crumble or tear the beef jerky into the mortar. Pound and mash it into a paste with the pestle.

2. Put the mashed jerky into the mixing bowl. Stir in the lard and cornmeal.

3. Chop the raisins as fine as possible on the cutting board. Stir the chopped raisins into the meat mixture.

4. With your hands, shape the mixture, a few tablespoons at a time, into cakes or bars.

5. Dry the cakes overnight on the wire rack.

6. Wrap each cake in plastic wrap. Store in the refrigerator.

MAKES 4–6 CAKES.

Beaded Necklace

Suddenly Laura shouted, "Look! Look!" Something bright blue
glittered in the dust. She picked it up, and it was a beautiful blue bead.
Laura shouted with joy. —CHAPTER 14

When Pa took Mary and Laura to visit the Indian camp, he first showed them where the campfires had burned and where the poles for their tents had been driven into the ground. They saw animal tracks, moccasin tracks, and the tiny fringe marks from a woman's leather skirt as she had bent low to stir a pot of stew.

But that was all forgotten when Laura spied the blue bead in the dust. She and Mary and Pa spent the rest of the afternoon collecting beads the Indians had left behind. Later Mary and Laura strung the beads onto a thread for a necklace for Baby Carrie.

The Osage wore bead necklaces too. They would wear several at a time, some tied close around their necks and a few longer ones.

To make a beaded necklace, you will need:

Ruler	*Embroidery needle*
Embroidery floss or heavy thread	*Small beads of various colors*
Scissors	*(available in craft stores)*

1. Measure a piece of heavy thread to the length you desire for your necklace (24 to 30 inches is about the right length). Cut the thread.

2. Thread the needle and tie a knot about 3 inches from one end of the thread.

3. Pick up each bead with the point of the needle and slide the bead over the needle onto the thread, all the way down to the knot. (If the knot is too small to hold the bead on securely, put the needle through the bead again to stitch it on.)

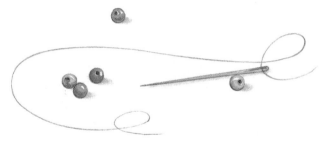

4. String as many beads onto the thread as you wish, in any combination of colors, until you come to the last 3 inches of thread.

5. Put the needle through the last bead again to stitch it onto the thread, then tie a knot in the thread. Cut the thread and remove the needle.

6. Tie the ends of the necklace together and slip it over your head.

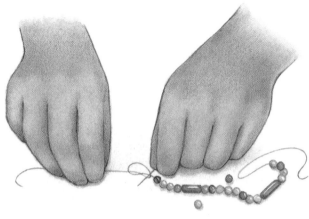

PRAIRIE ACTIVITIES

Beaded Bag

All that afternoon they hunted for beads
in the dust of the Indian camp. —CHAPTER 14

The Osage women also sewed beads in patterns on their buckskin clothing, their moccasins, or the little bags of deerskin they tied around their waists. They found inspirations for their designs in nature—birds, leaves, flowers, and vines.

To make your bead design, you will need:

Chalk or pencil   *Thread*
Small cloth bag or a square of cloth   *Sharp needle*
Scissors   *Small colored beads*

1. Use the chalk to lightly draw the design you want onto the cloth.

2. Cut a length of thread about 24 inches long. Thread the needle and tie a knot at the end of the thread.

3. From the underside of the cloth, push the point of the needle through the beginning of your design.

4. Put a bead on the needle, then pull the thread up through the cloth and the bead, keeping the bead close to the cloth. Stick the needle back into the cloth as close to the bead as possible.

5. Skip a thread in the cloth, then bring the needle up again. Repeat the process until the lines of the design are outlined with beads and thread.

6. Knot the end of the thread on the underside of the cloth. Cut off the excess thread.

The Blue Juniata

Ma's voice and the fiddle's music softly died away.
And Laura asked, "Where did the voice of Alfarata go, Ma?"
—CHAPTER 18

Written in 1844 by Mrs. Marion Dix Sullivan, this song tells the story of an Indian maiden named Alfarata remembering her sweetheart, a bold warrior. They lived near the Juniata River that flows through the Allegheny Mountains in Pennsylvania.

Moderately

Wild roved an In - dian maid, bright Al - fa - ra - ta,

Where flow the wa - ters of the blue— Ju - ni - a - ta.

Strong and true my ar - rows are in my paint - ed quiv - er,

Swift goes my light ca - noe a - down the ra - pid riv - er.

(Above) Laura around 1917, at the age of fifty.

(Opposite) Rose Wilder Lane in 1921.

9

Little House on the Prairie

The Book and Beyond

Laura Ingalls Wilder did not think about writing *Little House on the Prairie* or any of the other Little House books until she was nearly sixty years old. By then she and her husband, Almanzo, were semi-retired on their farm, Rocky Ridge, near Mansfield, Missouri.

One summer afternoon in 1923 Laura was wandering through a meadow at Rocky Ridge. She saw a wild sunflower, picked it, and held it close to her face. Later she recalled, "As I looked into its golden heart such a wave of homesickness came over me that I almost wept. I wanted Mother, with her gentle voice and quiet firmness; I longed to hear Father's jolly songs and to see his twinkling blue eyes; I was lonesome for the sister with whom I used to play in the meadow, picking daisies and wild sunflowers. Across the years, the old home and its love called to me and memories of sweet words of counsel came flooding back."

Pa had died over twenty years earlier, in 1902. In the spring of 1924 Ma died, and four years later Mary died. Both were buried alongside Pa in De Smet. Laura's memories continued to "flood back," and she felt more strongly than ever that her family's stories should be told, partly as a kind of memorial to Pa, Ma, and Mary. Her daughter, Rose, already an established author, encouraged her to write them down.

Finally, Laura opened a "Fifty Fifty" tablet of paper and began to write down her stories. Her first manuscript was called *Pioneer Girl*. In it Laura told about her experiences growing up on the midwestern prairies. When she finished it, she sent it to Rose, who took it to several publishers in New York. All of them turned it down.

Through the years Laura revised and rewrote the manuscript, and in 1931 it was accepted for publication by the children's department at the Harper & Brothers publishing house. At the time the country was in the grip of the Great Depression, and publishers were reluctant to publish new books. However, the editor of Laura's book realized that this was the kind of book the public was looking for—"that miracle book that no depression could stop." Harper & Brothers asked Helen Moore Sewell, a well-known artist of the era, to illustrate the book. In 1932 *Little House in the Big Woods* was published to immediate success.

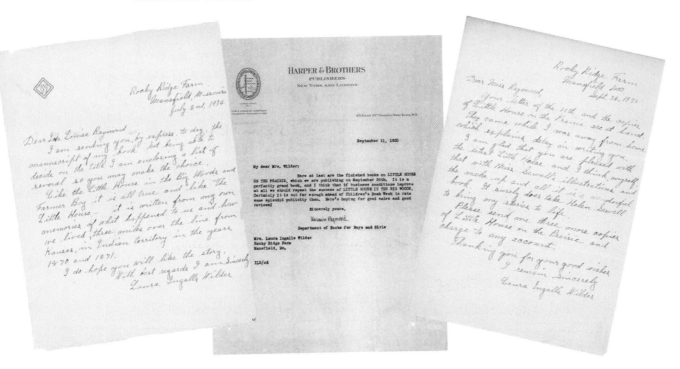

Letters to and from Laura and her publisher, Harper & Brothers.

Laura was more surprised than anyone else that her stories were so widely loved. Harper & Brothers wanted her to write another book, and readers did too. "Children who read it wrote to me begging for more. I was amazed because I didn't know how to write. I went to little red schoolhouses all over the west and I was never graduated from anything," Laura said.

At age sixty-five Laura had become a famous author. She started to write another book; this time she wrote about Almanzo's boyhood in Malone, New York. She called the book *Farmer Boy*.

Still, readers wanted more about the little pioneer girl Laura Ingalls. So Laura took out her paper tablets and pencil and began her third and most beloved book, *Little House on the Prairie*.

Helen Sewell illustration of Mary and Laura.

Although she had been only two years old when her family made their covered-wagon journey to Kansas, she remembered well the stories that Ma and Pa had told of their lives there—building the log cabin, digging the well, Mr. Edwards crossing the creek to bring their Christmas presents, and the long wagon rides across the prairie. As she wrote, her own memories of that time emerged. "I have learned in this work that when I went as far back in my memory as I could and left my mind there awhile, it would go farther back and still farther, bringing out of the dimness of the past things that were beyond my ordinary remembrance."

Little House on the Prairie, also illustrated by Helen Sewell, was published in 1935. Readers adored it and reviewers raved about it. A. J. Eaton wrote in *The New York Times*: "Mrs. Wilder has caught the very essence of pioneer life, the satisfaction of hard work, the thrill of accomplishment, safety and comfort made possible through resourcefulness and exertion. She draws, too, with

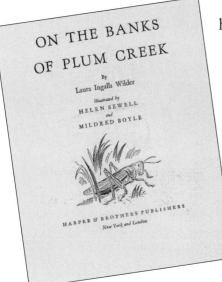

humor and understanding, the picture of a fine and courageous family, who are loyal and imaginative in their relationships with one another. Eight-to-ten year olds will find the book of absorbing interest."

Laura went on to write five more Little House books after *Little House on the Prairie*: *On the Banks of Plum Creek*, *By the Shores of Silver Lake*, *The Long Winter*, *Little Town on the Prairie*, and *These Happy Golden Years*, all illustrated by Helen Sewell with the assistance of Mildred Boyle. Laura's books were very popular and won awards; the last five were named Newbery Honor Books.

Shortly after World War II ended, Harper & Brothers decided to reissue *Little House on the Prairie* and the other Little House books with new illustrations and a new design, as size of the books varied and they contained relatively few illustrations. They selected Garth Williams, an up-and-coming children's book artist who had already received much recognition for his illustrations of E. B. White's *Stuart Little*, to be the new illustrator.

Before illustrating Laura's books, Williams spent several years traveling to each of the Little House sites and he visited with Laura and Almanzo at their farm in Missouri. The new editions were released in 1953 to much acclaim, and Laura herself noted, "Laura and Mary and their folks live again in these illustrations." His softly colored cover illustrations and

(Above) Title page for Laura's fourth book.

(Right) Laura and Almanzo in 1942.

charcoal-pencil drawings have been identified with Laura's books ever since. The new editions brought Laura even more attention and fame, but despite her success, she continued to lead much the same quiet kind of life she had always led.

Laura died on February 10, 1957, three days after her ninetieth birthday and almost eight years after Almanzo died. People around the world grieved her passing. After her death Laura's story continued to be told. Her diary describing the trip she and Almanzo and Rose made from De Smet to Mansfield in 1894 was published in 1962. In 1971 *The First Four Years*, which tells of the early years of Laura and Almanzo's marriage, was published. And *West from Home*, a collection of letters Laura wrote to Almanzo when she was visiting Rose in San Francisco, was published in 1974.

Also in 1974 a television series based on Laura's Little House books debuted. It starred Michael Landon as Pa, Karen Grassle as Ma, Melissa Gilbert as Laura, and Melissa Sue Anderson as Mary.

(Above, right) Garth Williams in 1986.

(Left) Garth Williams's covers for *Little House on the Prairie, Little House in the Big Woods,* and *On the Banks of Plum Creek.*

Laura autographing her books in Springfield, Missouri, in 1952.

Although the title of the program was *Little House on the Prairie*, it was set in Walnut Grove and featured the stories from the years Laura wrote about in *On the Banks of Plum Creek* and beyond, as the girls grew up. Not all the stories on the television program were taken from Laura's books, however. In the last years of the series, especially, more and more scripts departed from the original stories and biographical details about the Wilders and Ingallses to reflect more "modern" themes. The series ended in 1983, but reruns are shown today.

And today fans can visit the site of Laura's little log cabin on the prairie. In 1977 a replica of the little one-room cabin was built on the original site by a group of volunteers, following Laura's description of the cabin in her book. (To find it, visitors can follow U.S. Highway 75 southwest of Independence toward Wayside. Signs are posted with directions along the way.)

Although Laura's real little log cabin disappeared from the Kansas prairie years ago, her spirit continues to live on. The books written about Laura, the sites, and of course her own novels all contribute to a greater understanding of the world of this Missouri farmwife who finally realized that she had led "a very interesting life."

Bibliography

Anderson, William. *Laura Ingalls Wilder: A Biography*. New York: HarperCollins, 1992.

——, compiler. *Laura's Album. A Remembrance Scrapbook of Laura Ingalls Wilder*. New York: HarperCollins, 1998.

Catlin, George. *Letters and Notes on the North American Indians*. New York: C. N. Potter, 1975. (First published in London, 1841.)

Charbo, Eileen Miles. *A Doctor Fetched by the Family Dog: Story of Dr. George Tann, Pioneer Black Physician*. Springfield, Mo.: Independent Publishing, 1984.

Collins, Carolyn Strom, and Christina Wyss Eriksson. *My Little House Crafts Book: 18 Projects from Laura Ingalls Wilder's Little House Series*. New York: HarperCollins, 1998.

——. *The World of Little House*. New York: HarperCollins, 1996.

Evans, David Allan. *What the Tallgrass Says*. Sioux Falls, S.D.: Augustana College, The Center for Western Studies, 1982.

Garson, Eugenia, compiler and editor. *The Laura Ingalls Wilder Songbook: Favorite Songs from the "Little House" Books*. New York: Harper & Row, 1968.

Kurtis, Wilma, and Anita Gold. *Prairie Recipes and Kitchen Antiques*. Chicago: Bonus Books, 1993.

Marcy, Randolph B. *The Prairie Traveler. A Hand-book for Overland Expeditions, with Maps, Illustrations, and Itineraries of the Principal Routes Between the*

Mississippi and the Pacific. Originally published in 1859 by the War Department. Bedford, Mass.: Applewood Books, 1993.

Mathews, John Joseph. *The Osages: Children of the Middle Waters.* Norman, Okla.: University of Oklahoma Press, 1961.

——. *Wah'Kon-Tah: The Osage and the White Man's Road.* Revised edition. Norman, Okla.: University of Oklahoma Press, 1968.

Raphael, Ralph B. *The Book of American Indians.* New York: Arco Publishing, 1973.

Sherwood, Leon A. *The Spirit of Independence. Official Centennial History, Independence, Kansas, 1870–1970.* Independence, Kans.: Tribune Printing, 1970.

Smith-Baranzini, Marlene, and Howard Egger-Bovet. *USKids History: Book of the American Indians.* Boston: Little, Brown, 1994.

Verrill, A. Hyatt. *Our Indians: The Story of the Indians of the United States.* New York: G. P. Putnam's Sons, 1935.

Wilder, Laura Ingalls. *By the Shores of Silver Lake.* New York: Harper & Bros., 1939.

——. *Little House in the Big Woods.* New York: Harper & Bros., 1932.

——. *Little House on the Prairie.* New York: Harper & Bros., 1935.

——. *Little House on the Prairie.* Microfilm of unpublished manuscript. Columbia, Mo.: University of Missouri. Laura Ingalls Wilder Papers.

——. *On the Banks of Plum Creek.* New York: Harper & Bros., 1937.

Wissler, Clark. *Indians of the United States.* Revised edition. Garden City, N.Y.: Doubleday, 1966.

Zochert, Donald. *Laura: The Life of Laura Ingalls Wilder.* Chicago: Henry Regnery, 1976.

Illustration Credits

viii: from the Laura Ingalls Wilder Home Association (hereafter referred to as LIWHA).

1: from LIWHA.

2: photographs of Laura and Rose from LIWHA; photograph of Almanzo from the Rose Wilder Lane Collection at the Herbert Hoover Presidential Library (hereafter referred to as HHPL).

3: photograph of the Wilder farmhouse from William Anderson; photograph of Laura and Almanzo from LIWHA.

9: from Leslie Kelly.

92: from HHPL.

93: from William Anderson.

94: from HarperCollins Publishers (hereafter referred to as HC).

95: from HC.

96: title page from HC; photograph of Garth Williams from William Anderson.

97: book covers from HC; photograph of Laura and Almanzo from LIWHA.

98: from HC.

Index